A Sketchy Life

By Kevin Paul

Library Learning Information

To renew this item call:

0115 929 3388

or visit

www.ideastore.co.uk

TOWER HAMLETS

Created and managed by Tower Hamlets Council

D1331803

PERA
Publishing

Enquiries should be addressed to
Percy Publishing
Woodford Green,
Essex. IG8 0TF
England.

www.percy-publishing.com

1st Published April 2015
1st Edition

ISBN: 978-0-9929298-5-5

Cover Design Copyright © 2015 Percy Publishing

Jules @ Philter photography Derby Photographic Artist
Front Cover Picture Copyright of Philter Photography

Percy Publishing is a Clifford Marker Associates Ltd Company

Print: Svet Print, d.o.o., Ljubljana

Dedication

I would like to dedicate this book to my wife Tara, who has been there from the start of all this madness, and has seen the ups and the downs and all the bits in between. Having the boys changed my life for the better and gave me a reason to live, and for this I thank you so much.

I love you more than life itself.

Note from Publisher.

On the development of this book it was decided to
release it as close to the Authors wordings as possible.

Introduction.

Some of you reading this book will probably think it's just full of me name-dropping about all the celebrities I have met and worked with. Well, you really could not be more wrong! When I decided to do it I wanted everybody to see where I come from and what I have achieved in my 36 years. I have been through a lot in that time and had some real lows. I wanted to show everybody who reads this that no matter where you come from or what you have been through, anybody can achieve what they want if they just work hard and have belief in themselves. I have tried to be as honest as I possibly can be. This may or may not be a good thing - you decide!

Please let me know on my twitter account @kp_est78.

Chapter 1

I was born in Bramley, Leeds on the 1st of June 1978 at St James's hospital. My dad was a plasterer and my mum worked in a curtain factory; they never really had much money.

I have two older half siblings from my mum's side - a brother called Mark, who is ten years older than me and a sister Lesley, who is 12 years older than me. I don't really know that much about them, as they lived back in the Midlands with my mum's mum. They weren't really the best behaved of kids - always in trouble with the Police. The first time I even knew they were my brother and sister was when I was about 10. I never really saw much of them growing up, and I always thought I was an only child. I don't recall much about growing up in Leeds other than the house we lived in, 11 Landseer Grove in Bramley and the first school I ever went to up there.

I hated school even as far back as then. I never really ly fitted in with any of the other kids. One thing I do remember about it was being sick down the back of some kid's head. I got sent home at dinner time and I remember I had a small parcel waiting for me. It was a Star Wars figure, Admiral Ackbar and I was so happy with it.

My dad's only problem was his need to go to the pub all the time. He would go out to work first thing in the morning and as soon as he finished would go to the pub; then come home, have his tea and go back out again. It hurt my mum because she obviously loved him, but she was on her own up there without any family, as they were all back down in the Midlands. In the end she made the decision to leave him over it, and in 1982 we moved to the Midlands to be with my mum's side of the family.

I often went back up to see my dad and my gran and grandad though, and I will never forget their old house, 147 Granville Road in Bramley. They would always have a KitKat ready for me. I really liked my grandad - he was a lovely old man. He would repeat what he said to me so many times because he forgot what he had told me, or he would fall asleep half way through telling me something! They used to enjoy watching Brookside together, as he was from Liverpool.

I don't really remember much about when we moved away from my dad or how I felt about it, but I do remember the first flat we lived in. It was on Hastings Road in Swadlincote, and it was horrible - so cold, dirty and damp. My mum got really sick from living there, which I only found out when I was older. Life was not good for us back then. None of my mum's side of the family had much going for them; they were all pretty poor to be honest.

I will never forget putting some string around my

tooth and hooking it onto the door to pull it out while watching Knight Rider! I must have been about 6 at the time and it's about my only memory of that place.

I soon started at a junior school in Swadlincote. I still never really fitted in with the other kids or ever really made friends with them, and back then I was about the only kid from a broken home. I would watch all the other kids getting picked up by their dads or mums, but I never really had that growing up. My mum needed to work to keep us both going, so I was picked up by my nan who I never really had a bond with - she was very much all for my brother.

All I ever really wanted back then was a happy, normal family with a mum and dad to come back to. My dad stayed living in Leeds, so I never really got to see him much when I was young. When I did go up it would normally end up in the pub, then we would go pick up a curry on the way home. I can't really remember when it was that my mum met somebody new, but he was called Harold and he was such a nice guy. He was only short, so I would wear his 501 jeans when I was about 9 or 10. He had a really good job in Saudi Arabia, and in 1987 we ended up moving in with him in his house on Chiltern Road in Swadlincote. I have a lot of good memories from back then.

Christmas was always good. Harold would get me all the best presents and everything I ever asked for; all the family would come over and we all watched Only Fools and Horses. It started to feel more like a happy family for the first time in a long time. I was still not going to school though, and hadn't really made friends with anybody.

When I got home I would spend most of the time behind a bed that was on its side in the spare room. I would hide behind it and play with my toys or draw stuff - drawing was always my way of switching off from my life. I would sit there and doodle and just be zoned out. From a young age I always wanted to create things; I would fantasise about creating a working engine out of matchsticks and all sorts of other ideas that were going round in my head. I just loved to design things. The times I did decide to show up for school I would switch off and just day dream about life and the things I wanted to make.

I remember once I was sat in class daydreaming and wondered what would happen if the fire alarm went off. The next thing I knew I could hear the alarm. At first I thought it was just in my head because I was thinking about it, but then I realised it had actually gone off and it freaked me out a bit.

I had finally made a friend of this lad called Marc Edwards. He was one of the popular kids, so I found it odd that he wanted to hang out with me. I always felt a bit jealous of his upbringing; he had a mum and a dad there for him every day before and after school and his mum would get him ready - all the things I never got when growing up. I understand that now, after having kids of my own; my mum wasn't there because she was making sure money was coming in to clothe and feed us. I would do anything to protect my kids and give them the best I can in life.

Back to school, and my spelling was really bad. Letters just didn't make sense to me, and in those days nobody really understood what being dyslexic was. I was just made to feel like I was thick and was given books that were for kids younger than I was. They were awful - I will never forget them. They were called 'Fuzzbuzz' and I fucking hated them. It was so humiliating and the other kids were cruel at that age. I've always felt that my reading ability has held me back so much in life. I was a bit of a fuck-up back then. Until I was about 10 I had a problem with wetting the bed; my mum tried everything to stop it but nothing worked. I ended up getting hypnosis from the doctor and it never happened again. It was amazing.

I started to get into music around that time. I loved it all in the 80s - the music was just so feel-good - but I really got into a band called Bros. I loved everything about them, from the way they dressed to the London back-drop in their videos. I asked my dad if he could take me down to London for the weekend and when he said he would it was amazing! I loved it from the first second I got there. The bridges over the Thames, the buildings, the streets - I loved everything about the place and I felt at home there. Swadlincote was a bit backwards; it was such a small town, just for locals. I hated it! I remember asking my dad to take me into all the shops that Bros would get their clothes from and I got some of the Union Jack boxer shorts they wore. I even went as far as having my hair done like them and putting bottle caps on my shoes so I was the same.

***

I found myself drawing all the time by the age of 11. I would even draw on the beer mats in the pub when I was sat there with my dad. I wasn't like the other kids my age; I suppose I felt like I had to grow up faster because of being alone with my mum - almost like a protector, especially as I got older. I even pierced my own ears with a needle; back then it was seen as being gay to have both ears done, but I really didn't give a fuck. Whenever I was up in Leeds visiting Dad I would get my clothes from there because it was by far more up to date with fashion than Swadlincote. I think this made me stand out from the other kids too, but I didn't care; I was passionate about everything I did or wore, and when I've got my mind set on something there is no changing it. I will never forget the Unicorn, the pub my dad used to go to. The landlord Ken and his wife Judy were always really nice to me; my dad would have me do cartoon drawings of his friends, which always went down well.

***

In around 1989 Harold and my mum moved to Number 12 Trinity Grove. It was a really nice house - a new build on a new estate filled with lots of families. (I must have been about 11 at the time because I was about to change schools to go to secondary school, and I was enrolled at a place called the Pingle School in Swadlincote.) I have some really good memories of living there; for one thing we were some of the first people up there to have cable TV. Every Sunday morning I would sit drawing while my mum would make dinner with Radio 2 Classics on in the background. I remember the guy next door getting a Walkman. It was amazing - I had to get one! I used to collect some cards called Garbage Pail Kids; they were gross but funny, and I would sit and try to redraw them over and over again until I got them perfect. I think this was the happiest part of my childhood by far. Every Christmas all the family would come over and there would always be a family party.

I remember Marc getting a pair of Puma trainers one day; I loved them and I had to get some. I would draw them and keep drawing them over and over till I got a pair. It must have been where my love for trainers began and from that point on I always had the top trainers out. It was good when I went up to visit Dad because they had amazing trainer shops up there. The first pair I ever wanted was the Nike Air Max 90; they looked so cool it was like they had a spirit level in the bottom of them. I had to get a pair, but I looked everywhere for them and couldn't find them anywhere. Instead I ended up getting a pair of trainers called SPX, a gold and white boot. They looked really cool! When I wore them for school nobody knew what they were because it wasn't until about 6 months later that they finally came out in Swadlincote.

Every Sunday night I would watch a TV show called Spitting Image; I loved it and I would try to redraw the people on it all the time. It was the only good thing about a Sunday because I knew that the next day it was back to school. I hated secondary school. I was always put in the thick kids' class because they didn't know how to deal with me. Obviously I know now it was my own fault; if I'd always gone to school and paid attention then things might have been a little easier, but every day I would try my hardest to get out of doing things or going to classes.

In the summer Harold would always take us abroad on holiday. It was nice we were getting family holidays, but I was really shit in the sun. I would get really bad sun-stroke, faint and burn. One year we went away and I burnt my back so badly it came up in big blistering bubbles - it hurt so much! We tried all the pills and potions from the chemist's but nothing soothed it, so my mum ended up putting cold water soaked sanitary towels all over my back to try to help. It was so embarrassing! I looked a complete twat - it made me look like I had a hunch back.

***

My mum ended up leaving Harold in 1990 when I was around 12. It turned out he was being a bit of a cock to my mum by then. He would have little tantrums about the silliest of things - like his dinner not being ready, that type of stuff. I will never forget that up until that point me and my mum would always say 'I love you' before bed, but it never happened again after we left Trinity Grove. We ended up having to stay with my auntie Sandra and her husband for a while. She was married to an Indian man called Mowie who would make the best home-made curries. My auntie would get my cousin John ready for school, and it was the first time I was properly around that family life-style. I liked it there, but it didn't last, as it wasn't long before my mum met somebody new.

His name was Phillip Lansdown and we ended up moving in with him in about '92. He seemed a nice guy at first, always trying to help everybody and always trying to be the funny man he thought he was, but the cracks soon started to show. It wasn't long before he was shouting at my mum or me. I got a dog when we first moved and I could hear him at night hitting it; I would hear it crying and there was nothing I could do to stop him - I was only 12 or 13 at the time. Then one day the dog disappeared. I knew he had done something with it but there was nothing I could do to prove it.

After my mum got her money from her divorce to Harold she got us a new home on Brook Street in Swadlincote. The only trouble was, that scumbag we were living with moved in too. I started to hate him: he was always shouting at my mum and trying to play mind games with people. None of the family liked him or would come around anymore. That was it - there were no more family Christmases for us. I can see now that she only put up with it so she could afford to look after me and pay the bills, but back then I didn't get it and I really hated everything about life. I would happily have gone to sleep and never woken up. I thought about running away to London so many times; it would even have been better up in Leeds with my dad. It got to the point that if ever this Phillip came into the room I would get an empty, low feeling inside of me. I hated that feeling.

I had no time for school or having any friends, I just wanted to be close to my mum to make sure she was safe. I had nobody to talk to about it all, or anybody there to help. I remember once he put a live spider in my lunch box for school and a bee under my pillow. He really was a total scumbag and I fucking hated the sight of him. He was a bully, but it was only kids and women he would do it to; he had a go at me once round the back of our house. I told him to go fuck himself and he tried to hit me, then when I pulled away he tried to hit me with a spade. He was just a nasty man. We was on electric cards in that house and I remember once it ran out in the dark and he made us sit for hours with no electric, just so he could try to play some tricks on me. In my head I would think about killing him - just sticking a knife right into his gutless heart - but I knew that was stupid and I could never get away with it. The only thing that would help comfort me was to draw things.

I remember going to work with my dad one day and I noticed one of his friends had an Elvis Presley tattoo. It was only a cartoon drawing but it looked really cool and as soon as I got back to the flat I tried to re draw it over and over again. I was 14 at the time and it was 1992, when the tattooing industry was a lot different to what it is now. Back then you would just pick a basic design from the wall and get it done, but there was still something that got me interested in it. My dad's old-fashioned; he hated them then, and he still does really. He thought everybody with tattoos was a scum- bag, gang members or prison lags! My brother and sister had been tattooed, so as soon as I got home I asked my brother all about it and he told me how he got tattooed when he was in prison. They would use an old shaver or a motor out of a motorised toy car and an old Allen key and a pen. Somebody my brother knew gave me an old catalogue full of tattoo designs that a tattooist friend of his had left round their house. Something in me lit up with excitement. I had such love for the art of tattooing from that day forward that I would draw tattoo designs day and night, and even my school books had them all over their covers.

I made my own machines from stuff I would steal from school. Then I sat at home one night and had a go on myself; I did a little cross on my finger and a heart on my arm. It was really shit and I know now it was not a safe thing to do at all, but at the time I loved it. I just wanted to get a real one more than ever now. The guy that left the book was coming back to stay and tattoo at my brother's friend's house again. I just had to get something done, so I sold my stereo for £20 to the second hand shop. As soon as I got there I loved everything about it, from the hygienic smell to the look of the machines. When I had a look at all his designs I couldn't choose - I wanted everything - but I ended up picking a naked woman with a snake around her. I had it done on my lower right arm, and that was it for me! As soon as the needle hit my skin I knew I wanted to tattoo; then as soon as I left I wanted to go back and get more. I decided to try and sell anything I could to get more work done before he left. When I got home and my mum saw it she just said, "You stupid bastard!" and that was it.

I didn't really have much time for school after that. I knew what I wanted to do and school was not going to get it for me. My home life was still really shit; every day there was another fight with that scumbag, but I finally had something positive in my life to look forward to. Back then I would run away from things I didn't want to do - and that was a *lot*! I think that was the main reason I didn't go to school, but anyway my reading and writing were still really poor and I hated having to read out loud or write in front of people. I was so embarrassed I just ran away from it and I would not go in - that was unless I wanted to steal some more ink out of the art studio. I made friends with two of the kids in my class, though. They were both called Mark and not very bright, and they were from really poor families with criminal backgrounds.

Chapter 2

One day we spoke about going out robbing from the local toyshop after school. I planned it all out and told them what to do, and they got game boys and games in the first go, so we went back the next day and did the same. We got so good at it that I ended up taking them all over the place stealing everything we could, and we did it for months. I would take all the stuff to a local hang out and sell it to a lady who ran a club we used to go to.

They were not very bright lads, so I kept most of the money we got. I felt like planning all this was a bit of a skill I had, and I got a bit of a buzz from doing it too. I think it was just a distraction from all the shit in my home life. I was still only around 14 at the time and we never got caught doing anything; we could've done it for longer I'm sure.

I didn't see it at the time, but I think that was the first sign of me going down the wrong path. The two Marks lived in a place called Newhall, just outside of Swadlincote. It wasn't a very nice place to live; most of it was run down and a lot of the lowlife type of families lived there. I would hang around there after school, and as my brother also lived there I would spend a lot of time around his - I would go everywhere with him. One day I was up the park in Newhall and one of my brother's friends offered me a fag. It was a roll-up and I didn't think much to it at the time, but it was a cannabis joint he had given me. It didn't really have much effect on me to start with and back then I just wanted to be the big man and look cool in front of my brother and his friends. It was fucking stupid, I know that now, but back then that's who I was. I started to like the feeling of taking cannabis; it took my mind off my troubles and made being at home easier to handle. I would smoke it most days from about the age of 15 and I started to hang out with some of the local dealers – I found I got on with them all so well, and they had an even shittier life than I did. I soon started to deal a little cannabis to the kids at school. The thing about living in Swadlincote was that for most people it was all about looking big and hard. That's what seemed important to them, and I was no different. I think my brother could see I was going the way he did when he was young. I would go round his for my tea most days and he would drop me off home after; some nights he would tell me tales of what he used to get up to, and how he ended up in Children's Homes growing up. They were not nice places. They would take his clothes off him to stop him breaking out, but he would still break out and steal a car and drive home. I can see now that he was trying to help me, but back then I just thought it was cool to do that type of thing.

***

I remember when School sent me on a week's work experience at a plastic moulding factory, which I saw as a good time to get more tattoos. I went to a guy who worked from his house in Swadlincote - my brother showed me where he lived. I got some skulls up my left arm to cover the little shit heart I did myself when I built my first machine. I just loved getting tattooed; I loved everything about the trade.

It was really hard to get tattoo magazines back then when there was no internet to view things and not that many people were into them. The school had just about given up on me by then; I hardly ever went, and when I did I would just end up in trouble. I tattooed some of the scummy kids at school round one of their houses. It was not a good thing to do, I know that now, but I was a kid. I just wanted to tattoo, and there was no other way for me to learn. One day I went in to school and the head spotted me in the hall and asked me to follow him. I went back to his office and he said, "You know why you're here don't you?" I thought he was on about me getting a tattoo, so I asked was it about that. But he didn't even know about it - he was on about some other kid getting a little cross tattooed by me on his arm. I said I never did it and that they couldn't prove I had. In the end they kind of just stopped caring about me turning up any more.

When I got kicked out of school one of the first things I did to make money was shop lift. There was a local Sports Centre in Swadlincote with a shop inside it that sold ski coats and that sort of stuff. It was all high end - the coats started at around £150, going up to about £400. I started taking a coat a day but within a month or so I was lifting 3 or 4 coats a time, and I would get anything from £75 to £150 a coat.

There was a local woman who ran a pub in Swad who would buy everything I got and move it on fast from the pub. I kind of got off on the buzz of it all: that fear of getting caught just made me want to do more. I never really wanted this for my life, but I had no education and nothing going for me – it seemed my only option. Before I started this book I had come to look down on people like that, but going over all this as I write has reminded me this is the life I come from too. Most people don't want to live like that; they just don't have much choice. I feel really lucky that I got a break in life, a chance to do something with myself, and that I always had the drive to be a tattooist to keep me going. In Burton on Trent there was only one tattooist to go to and everybody knew him. I really wanted to get more work done but I was still only 15 at the time, so I thought I would try my luck with him. I looked a lot older than I really was and I already had tattoos, so in my head I thought I might get away with it. I always wanted a little red devil on my bum - I don't know why, but I did. It was always full in there though, and I ended up picking the Fantasia Mickey Mouse. I had it on my lower arm and it cost me £13. I got on with him really well and I began spending a lot of time in there. I would draw up stuff for him to tattoo on the clients as they came in, and I had turned 16 by then so I didn't have to deal with school shit anymore.

***

My home life was still really bad. Mum was still with

that scumbag, but as I was getting older and starting to get to know a lot of nasty people he would watch what he said in front of me.

I would get picked up most nights and go down town and hang out with some of the local gangster kinds that lived around there. It seemed so cool at the time and there were so many flash cars that would come down and hang out with us. Some of them were part of a big car crime ring. They would focus mainly on stealing RS Turbos and Cosworths, as they brought in more money when they were broken up for parts.

The guys we worked with used to have mirror cars of the ones we would steal, so what we would do was take replica plates and tax discs with us. When we found a car that matched we would swop the plates and tax disk, so to a police patrol they would be completely legit if it was rung up. Tax, insurance - the lot. Easy!

I started going to Manchester most nights with one of the lads. He would steal a Vauxhall Calibra Turbo and we would drop it off to these guys up there. They had a plan: it was always a black or silver car he would take, as the guys that would buy the cars drove those colours; we had copy plates made up, so if we ever got pulled we could just give their details.

There was always a chance of getting caught, and I really got off on the buzz. You could see these guys were really nasty fuckers, and I was only young at the time and really out of my depth. I would spend all the money I could make on getting tattooed. I was almost covered by now; I'd had most of my arms and all of my back done. I just couldn't wait to go back for more!

When we were looking for cars to steal we would go

to car shows - mostly Ford. All the cars would have a list of every mod they had on them, even down to the alarms, and it was so easy to take. We would make a note of the number plates of the cars we wanted, and when we got back we would get a friend who had a car garage to run the plates to find out where the car was based. When we went to get it we would go down a day or so before to try find out who owned the cars. Some of them turned out to be fucking nut cases and they would come running out the house after you.

We finally got it down to a tee. There would be 3 of us go down: one would drive the car, the other would take the stolen car and I would stand watch, keeping an eye out for the owner. It was so cool to see how fast he could take a car; he would take a steel pole with him to break the steering lock and then he did the whole thing in about 3 minutes. When I went with them they always give me £100. I was only about 16 at the time and I thought I was so cool doing it. Looking back on it now I was so lucky I didn't get caught; every last one of the other guys ended up behind bars.

There was this one car that they tried to get but every time they did the owner would come running out with a bat. Then one night this lad asked how much they would give him if he got them that car. They didn't believe he could, but they said they would happily give him 2 grand. I was down with them when this lad went to get it. He just walked up to the door and knocked on it, and the guy who opened it was a big cunt - must have been 6 foot 4. The lad was about 5foot 10 and he just got in the guy's face and started shouting at him with a bar in his hand. He said, "Give me the fucking car keys!" The guy shit himself and just gave him his keys. I could not believe what I was seeing - he just took the car, told him not to phone the police for two hours, and then drove off in his car!

***

I walked in the house one day and I could hear Phil shouting at my mum, and I could see he was in the bathroom. I had the little steel poker thing for the coal fire on me, as I used it for protection when I was out, (I stuck it down the back of my trousers). I kicked the bathroom door open and it knocked him flying into the bath. My mum ran out of the room and phoned the police; he came running out after me and I stood my ground but he managed to get me to the floor. This day had been a long time coming. I wanted to smash his fucking head in and I give it my all, but my mum get kept getting in the way. He tried to hit me but I just kept blocking it, then I pulled out the poker and hit him across his legs. It took him down. He ran outside to get a brick and tried to run back in and get me with it, but my mum slammed the door on him and he just chucked it towards me through the glass. Glass went flying and some shards got me in the face. He reached in and tried to grab me through the broken window; he cut all my neck up and I was covered in blood, but just as this was happening the Police turned up and arrested him. I had great joy in sticking two fingers up at him as they drove off with him, and after that we didn't see anything of him for about a week. It was so refreshing for the first time in all these years to feel safe in my own home, but then he turned up again one night. The back door had been left open and he just walked in and started shouting that he had a gun. He made us sit down while he shouted and raved for about an hour and then went to nip to his car, so I jumped up, locked the door and called the police. He soon took off, but he said I would pay for what I had done; he even tried paying a local drug dealer to beat me up, but luckily I knew him so he told me first.

I had to watch my back at all times and I would walk my mum to work to make sure she was safe. I was 16. I shouldn't have been doing those things or living like that, I should have been going out with friends. He finally went to court for what he did. Unfortunately he didn't get sent down for it, but he got a big fine to pay and he had to stay away from us or he would be prosecuted.

This was some good news, but then I realised my mum would now not have as much money to pay the bills and would be struggling.

I started to try and help as much as possible. I even got a job as a builder's labourer. I fucking hated it but I stuck at it for about two months. I just wasn't up for doing these types of jobs - I loved to design stuff, I'm a really creative person - so I ended up leaving and went back to what I knew best: crime. I would get involved with the local dealers and I was really good at shop lifting.

I made a fold-up steel frame that I used to hide in the bus park behind the trees; late at night I would go get it out, feed it through the letter boxes, hook things up and feed it out again. It worked really well and I got away with it for a long time.

I got asked one day if I knew anybody who could burn out their car so they could report it to their Insurance as stolen. I thought yes, I could do that. The guy handed me £200 to do it and gave me a spare key, so that night I rolled the car down the road out the way and then started it up and drove it to some fields not too far away. I put petrol all over it – inside too. Trust me, you don't understand how fast it goes up! I nearly shit myself, it went up with such a bang. I had a friend waiting to pick me up and I had to run really quick to get in the car. My heart was beating so fast! I really got off on the buzz of doing stuff like this. Anyway, we had gotten away with it and we ended up doing it 3 or 4 more times over the year: it was a fast track to easy money. Back then I would do anything to make money, and I was mainly doing it to help my mum so I could slip money into her handbag just to help as much as I could.

It was around 1994 by now, and the rave scene was kicking in big time. I remember the first rave I ever went to. It was in Burton upon Trent and Carl Cox was playing it. I had been given an acid tab and an E tablet; it was such a weird feeling to have - it makes you think that you can see stuff when it's not really there. Most of the people there were sitting around rolling spliffs, and there were so many beautiful girls at these things. I remember sitting down next to this girl and she asked me if I wanted a joint. I said yes, and then the next minute she pulled her bottoms down a bit and pulled some cannabis out of her knickers. I caught a little glimpse of her minge and I didn't know where to look. Everybody was so kind to each other at raves

- nothing like it is now when you go out. When we left we walked back over the bridge out of town and I was hallucinating so badly I thought I could see the Titanic coming towards me. I was really losing it at this point so I tried to look the other way, but that was no better - I thought I could see dead bodies in the water. The bridge was only about a 5 minute walk but it felt like it took hours to walk over that night. I don't know why after that, but I kept going back and doing it most weekends. I really didn't have anything going for me in life; I thought this was about as good as it was going to get.

I was still doing the car thing too, dropping off the stolen cars in Manchester. We got on with those guys really well and we would go to parties they would have up there. It was the first time I ever saw a gun and I will never forget it. We were in a club with a couple of the guys from up there and I could see the inside of one of their coats. I thought I could see a gun in the inside pocket but didn't know for sure, so just forgot about it. When we left I got into a car with one of them. I was staying in Leeds that night, so he said he would drop me off but he had to go do a little deal on the way. He took his coat off when he got in the car and put it in the back.

He had to meet the guy in Leeds back of the train station, under a bridge. When we got there it must have been about 3 in the morning, and he told me to stay in the car while he went to meet him. He went in the back, pulled out a bag and stuck it in his back pocket, and then he pulled out a gun from his coat; he said he was taking it just in case, as he had never worked with this guy before. The rave scene was quite a good thing back then – even the drugs were cleaner – but there were a lot of dealers being robbed by other dealers at gun-point, and when he got out I didn't have a clue what was going to happen. He was gone for about 20 minutes; I couldn't hear anything from the car or see where he went, but when he came back he chucked me £50 and said, "That went well!" laughing to himself. I knew I was getting involved with people I shouldn't be, and I was kind of scared but thought it was really cool at the same time. I wanted to brag about it, but knew I could not say anything. I know now it was a really silly thing to do; I would absolutely hate for any of my kids to do anything that I did when they grow up. Drug taking was a common thing by then. It was always around and easy to get hold of; I was turning into a not so nice person, and when I look back now it doesn't seem like I ever *was* that person.

I met two lads in 1997 called Carl and Keith and I got on with them really well from the start. We just had fun every day, and spent most of our time getting stoned and making money any way we could. There was this guy who lived up the road from us. Nobody liked him - he was a registered paedophile. His windows were always getting put in and he would stand at them most nights watching what we were up to. He would go up to the phone box at the top of the street and phone the police telling tales on people, and some nights we would follow him up. I would block the door shut with him in there and we would all pick a corner and piss on him through the gaps in the door. I know it sounds bad now, but I was young and he was not a nice person at all. One night I walked past his house and he was stood out watching what we were doing, so I jumped over his fence and bear-hugged him up in the air, then flipped him upside down and put him in his wheelie bin. His legs were flapping around all over the place, and the twat was there for ages while we just sat over the road watching him. When the Police turned up they asked us if we did it; we said no, we just wanted to see how long it would take him to get out.

Another time, Carl and Keith went out stealing car stereos and we got pulled in by the Police. I was sat in the back of the car and I pushed my coat over them and squashed it under the seat. I pushed it as far under as I could with my feet so they didn't see what I was doing. They looked around the car but never picked up on what I'd done. We were so lucky to get away with it! Carl was very unbalanced. I remember him sticking a knife under a dealer's neck because he said something he didn't like. He didn't take shit from anybody, but we would never turn on each other; we always had each other's backs. I'd never had friends like that before. Keith was a mardy guy - it didn't take much to get him to flip. I would keep flicking him in the balls just to piss him off, taunting him all the time, but he never turned on me.

I would do anything I could do to make money other than get a job. I had some thick guys out stealing from catalogues, shops, or from anywhere we would be able get money from. When I think about it now I'm so embarrassed about what I used to be like. It really doesn't seem like that was me. One day me and Keith were out sorting some stuff out and there was this rich kid who was a bit older than us parked up down the road. He would always make comments when he drove past us. He was a right prick. Daddy had got him a Vauxhall Astra GTE - he always got what he wanted. When he came past us this day he made some comment as usual as he drove by. Then he pulled up down the road to pick his mate up, and he was still waiting for him as we went past. Keith just pulled him out the car and started smashing his head into the side of it. The lad's mate come running out, but he looked at me then did nothing. Keith really fucked him up - there was blood everywhere. He kicked him in the face about ten times and got blood all over his shoes; he could be a really nasty cunt when he wanted to be. Then we just walked away and carried on with what we'd been doing, but Keith was really hyped up after it. He saw this lad walking down the road, so he went up to him and said, "Give me your fucking shoes!" The lad tried to say no, but Keith just took them anyway. We couldn't afford to get pulled over after what just happened with one of us wearing blood stained shoes.

Every couple of weeks I would pull away from it all and go back round my brother's for a bit, and Carl had a flat in Newhall where we would hang out - it was on a street that everybody called 'Cannabis Court' which says it all really, doesn't it! Everybody knew where we lived, so if anybody ever wanted to get hold of us it was easy to do. One day two black guys pulled up the lad that would do our running around for us; when he got stopped by them they were in a big old Rover. They told him to come over to the car, and he stuck his head in at the window to be greeted with a gun in his face.

They told him to tell us to pack in what we were do-ing or they would stop it for us. I didn't react much, but Carl really wanted to get his own back. We didn't know who they were or where they were, but the lad who got the gun in his face come running in crying - it really scared him.

Chapter 3

I must have been 17 by now, and I didn't have anything going for me. I tried getting money from the Prince's Trust to set up a tattoo studio but they just didn't want to help.

One day I got this lad to give me a lift into town and somebody ran out on us trying to stop us. He turned in towards the kerb and it made the car flip across the other side of the road. We were only lucky a car wasn't coming, I climbed out and was in so much pain radiating around my shoulder and neck. I ended up in hospital all night and the next day I went to see a solicitor about the accident.

It was around this time that my mum met somebody new. His name was Keg, he was a nice guy and really down-to-earth. He would even have the odd joint with me before bed. It was nice to see my mum happy again too - it was one less thing for me to have to worry about.

One night we had a visit from two local dealers; when they walked in they locked the door behind them and took out the key; of course I knew something was wrong from that moment and I had a cold feeling shoot down my body. This was not going to end well - I thought I was going to die. Suddenly one of them swung a baseball bat at Keith but it missed him. I think if it had hit him, it would've killed him. The other lad had a knife. I could tell that Keith was wanting to smash his fucking head in and Carl kept a knife down the side of his chair. My heart was pounding; I knew this could end in a blood bath. I could see the dealers were on something - they didn't know what day it was. This just made them really unpredictable. Luckily things started to calm down, and after about 3 hours they got to the point of why they were there. One of them was saying somebody had broken into his flat and stolen all his drugs. They had it in their heads that it was us, but it was the first I had ever heard about it. I was always good at bullshitting people with blag, so I told them I thought I knew who had done it and they let me leave to go try find them. It was about 3 in the morning and it was the middle of the winter, I will never forget it - I just went home as fast as I could. I knew I had to get out of this shit life I had got myself into.

I started to think about how all I'd ever really wanted to do was tattoo people and draw, and I kept my head down for about a week or two. Then one day I had a meeting at the Job Centre about my benefits. When I was waiting I started to get a tightening feeling in my chest; the sensation was horrendous and I started to panic, thinking I was going to pass out. I didn't know what was happening so just got myself sorted and caught the bus home. After that I felt so low and down for a couple of days, but as soon as I got over it I went back round the flat to Carl and Keith.

Keith wasn't there, but there was a local hard nut that had come round. (I recognised him because he knew my brother's friend.) He asked us both if we could get a car stereo for him; we said yes, we were sure we could get anything he wanted. Then suddenly he got Carl by the throat: he had tricked us. It turned out his mum had hers stolen the night before and he told us to go round to his house that night with answers. He said if we didn't show up then there would be consequences: I knew he just wanted to give somebody a kicking over it.

We didn't want to risk not turning up, but when we got there he had 6 of his mates with him, and I knew it was not going to end well. One of them hit Carl in the face, but he just stood there and looked him straight in the eyes - Carl didn't care about a punch to the face, he wasn't right in the head. I kept planning what I would do if they tried that shit with me. In life I have always forward- planned what I would do as a reaction to what other people are doing. After a while of them going on at us, I asked them when it happened. It ended up being a night that I was at my brother's, which proved it couldn't have been me. I told him, since he knew my brother, to call him to confirm. When he came off the phone he said, "Right - it wasn't you. Get out of my sight!" and I was so relieved. I really think somebody or something was watching over me. I always seemed to come out ok from the shit places I got myself into.

***

The next day I started to get that same panic feeling I'd had the week before, and I ended up with a sickness bug which took me out for days. I'd had no drugs in my system for that past week, but I just got worse. Thinking about it now, I must have been coming down from all the drugs I had taken over the years. Obviously at the time I didn't realise what was going on, but the long term use of cannabis had left me with bad panic attacks. Anyway, one thing led to another and after about 4 months I still hadn't left the house. If ever I tried to go out I was stopped by one of these panic attacks. It really started to get me down, to the point where I even thought about taking my own life. Day and night it never left me; it felt like I was not even safe in my own body. I had no normal feeling left in me – I was just empty. I made an appointment at the doctor's but waiting around all the people in the reception area really freaked me out. Then when I did go in, the doctor didn't seem to care. I wasn't even told what was going on or why. The only thing that seemed to help me chill out a bit was drawing, and I spent hours drawing tattoo designs.

I only knew that the feelings I was getting were brought on by a terrible fear of passing out in public, and after about 6 months of it I ended up going for a brain scan at Derby Hospital. Going anywhere in public made me feel anguished - I hated it, and I was so down I really just wanted to end it all. As I was on benefits but never left the house I saved a lot of money, so I would get my mum to buy me loads of tattoo mags.

There weren't many magazines out back then, only two or three, but I started being fascinated by the demonic style of work being done. I didn't know at the time, but the work I liked was all by the same guy. His name was Paul Booth and he worked from a studio called Last Rites in New York City. After the hard up-bringing I'd had, I found this type of artwork helped me to get all the dark and negative feelings out of my head. The first drawing by him was a man being eaten by a massive fly. He had bunny slippers on. Then I saw a leg sleeve he did with demons and brains all over it - it was disgusting, but so cool at the same time, and I would try to redraw it over and over. He was one of the only people doing stuff like this at that time. Because of him black and grey really came on, and I found my own style of art starting to get darker after that.

***

I had been stuck in the house now for about 8 months, and I wasn't getting any better. Some nights I just wished I didn't have to wake up. I remember a lad I knew that hanged himself in the local park and I couldn't help but feel kind of happy for him. He was out of pain, and at the time I knew just how he felt. It's such a dark subject - depression and panic attacks - and people don't know how to approach it.

Something else I bought with the benefits money that was building up was a Staffordshire bull terrier. He was a little black and white male and I called him Pig. (I still couldn't leave the house, so my mum had to take him for his jabs and I hated it - I wanted to do all that stuff myself.) I didn't know at the time, but getting that puppy would end up saving my life. As the weeks went on I started to take him for walks just around the block at night until I slowly built myself up for taking him on longer walks and eventually out in the daytime when more people would be about.

I found having Pig really helped take my mind off it all, and after about 3 months I was starting to get back on my feet. I even found a little house just up the road from my mum's on Chapel Street in Church Gresley; it didn't have much in it, but it was a start. When I went back to the doctor's they told me that anything like caffeine would bring on the panic feelings, so I decided to cut out drinking anything but water. My life was slowly starting to come back and I started to hang out again with old friends like Keith.

One day I was walking down the high street in Swadlincote and I noticed a white Staffordshire bull terrier in one of the shop windows. I walked in to have a look and it turned out to belong to the girl who ran the shop. I got talking to her and she seemed nice, (she must have been about 19 and I was just about to turn 18.) I would pop in most days to say hi, and we got on really well. After about 3 weeks of talking things started to get a bit more full on, and one night after she locked up I walked her back to her car. We ended up having a little kiss and I told her I liked her, but the only problem with this was she still had a boyfriend. Anyway, we went on as we were for two or three more weeks.

***

I woke up one morning to a letter from my solicitors about the car crash I was in, saying I'd been made an offer and to come in for a meeting: I was really excited - I was expecting a couple of grand - but when I went in and they said they wanted to give me £20,000 I couldn't believe it. I had never seen that kind of money before - and it was totally legal! The girl from the shop finally ended up leaving her boyfriend and I asked her to move in with me.

On my 18th birthday I got the cheque in the post for £20,000. I couldn't wait to start spending it, and as soon as I could I drew out ten grand. The moment I got it we bought the best of everything - the biggest TV, a fast car, the lot. I gave my mum some to help her with her house, and after about a year we moved into our own place in Midway, just outside of Swadlincote. It was a nice sized ex council house and we made it a proper home. We decided to try for a baby, and it didn't take more than a couple of months or so before she fell pregnant. I was so happy. She was still running the shop in Swadlincote, as it was for her dad. He was really well off and ran a chain of shops all over the Midlands. I really liked her dad: he gave me a lot of his time and helped me see I could do better in life. He was like that father figure I never had.

When we went for the second scan we found out we were having a boy. I couldn't have been happier: I just wanted to give him a better life than I had growing up; I wanted to protect him and make sure I did right by him. At the time I was still selling stolen stuff from her dad's shop. It was a real money maker at the time but I didn't want this for my son and her dad was on about shutting the shop soon anyway, so I saw it as my opportunity to get a proper job. The only pitfall was, I had no qualifications and could hardly spell my own address.

I ended up in dead end jobs and I fucking hated it! The first one I got was at a place called Tyre Technics, which involved making tyres. I didn't mind it to start with and the money was ok. I would spend all my free time and money getting tattooed or buying tattoo magazines. After about 4 months they started to go under, so I had to find something fast, and I got a job in a local slaughterhouse. It was horrible! I only lasted 3 hours in there before I quit. Now I had nothing coming in. I knew I just had to take anything that came along, so I ended up with a job in a local plastic moulding company. I didn't mind that at first; the pay was shit but it was a job, and that was all that mattered. I knew I could do so much better for myself but just had no way of achieving it. All I'd ever wanted to do was draw and tattoo. I got really sick of brain-dead people who had worked where they were ever since leaving school and were now talking down to me. After about 3 months I ended up hating that job too.

We were parents by now with a little boy called Dennon who was everything I lived for. I just wanted him to have a good life.

I was now 21, and still didn't really have much going for me. We were finding it hard just to pay the bills, never mind anything else. Her mum and dad helped us out loads, but they shouldn't have had to and the stress of it all would be bound to show on our life as a couple. I ended up getting a job at Coors Brewery in Burton upon Trent and the missus got a job at a local petrol station. I think the damage had already been done with us before that point though, and I could tell something was wrong.

After about 4 months we were falling out a lot, but it really hurt to think that I might end up not being there for Dennon. I even remember confronting her to see if she had cheated on me; I was in tears at the thought of it. She said she would never do anything like that, but I just had a gut feeling there was more to it.

Then just after Christmas Day she told me she wanted to split up. It really broke me as a person: I loved the bones of her - she was the mother of my child - and I just didn't know what to do with myself. Half of me just wanted to shout at her but then the other half wanted to beg her to stay.

I ended up losing my job and going out and getting pissed. I hadn't had a drink in years. I was a total mess. We had to stay together for about a month before I could find somewhere else to live. I got a job at a place in Swad called Bennet's Pet Foods and shortly after I found a house just over the road from it, so everything was going ok. I was out all the time, and started to meet up with some guys I knew of from being around town. Some of them were ex-football hooligans; they loved to fight when they were younger, but they were all getting on a bit by this time. They were all in their 30s and had been left by their partners, so had started to go out down town all the time. One of the guys was also into his tattoos, and he lived across the road from my sister, so I spent most days there and we got on really well.

I was about ten years younger than the rest of them, but it didn't matter at all and we starting going out most nights. Thinking back about it, we were all just lonely and looking to meet somebody. I would drink a lot back then – get really badly drunk and then turn very arrogant and full of myself. Nobody could ever really say anything to me though, as I was always out with a bunch of nasty big guys that loved to fight.

One night there was a girl in a club we went into that was a barmaid in our local pub. I would have a chat when we went in and I could see she liked me but I never really did anything about it. When she came in the club I could see she was with her boyfriend - just a normal looking lad – but I could tell she wanted to come and chat. After about 2 to 3 hours she was getting pissed and I could see the boyfriend didn't like her talking to me, but he couldn't do shit with the people I was with. The club was getting really full by this point, and I took her to one side of the club and pinned her up against the wall. She couldn't wait to kiss me; she was like a leach sucking my face off, and I was on her for about 5 minutes. I ended up pulling her skirt to the side and sticking two fingers in her and she loved it, the dirty bitch. Everybody in the club could see what was going on. When I was done I turned around and her boyfriend was just stood there waiting for me to finish with her, and the guys I was with just started laughing.

The next morning I felt so bad about it all - I really didn't want to keep going out doing this shit, but I didn't have anything else in my life. The next week I went back to the same club and I saw her in there again. When her boyfriend noticed me his face went pale, and I could see what he was thinking [Not again!] Anyway, I ended up taking her to the side again - I didn't even want her, I just did it because I could. I know now it wasn't a nice thing to do but I was young back then and I didn't have a clue what life was about; I was really lonely and didn't know what to do with myself. Thinking about it, it's probably why Karma got me back with a cheating wife in the future. All I wanted was my family back. Coming from a broken family myself, that was the last thing I wanted for my son. His mother was ok to start with and she let me see Dennon most of the time. I found it really hard to talk to girls when I was out though, because I was only really used to my ex. It took me a long time to move on, and then after about 3 months she started wanting to spend time with me again. This really messed with my head, as I thought we would end up getting back together but we didn't it and it just made getting over her worse. After about 6 months I started to go on dates again, but I hated it. It was really hard for me, as I'm a really shy person and find it hard to make friends. My ex saw me out one night with a girl and she had a right go at me in front of them and chucked a drink at me. She hated seeing me moving on. Things were starting to go from bad to worse with us.

One day when I was round the house I found a second phone she had hidden in a drawer. When I looked at it I saw she was texting a lad I worked with. He was a right scumbag, and I wasn't happy; I didn't want Dennon around scum like that. We fell out over it all and she made it really hard to see him - even when it was his birthday she didn't let me see him - so I decided to go round to her mum and dad's. They tried to make out they weren't in, but I knew they were there. It really hurt that they would do this, as I looked up to them for so long, and they had helped me so much over the years.

The house that I ended up in was filled to the brim with damp and mould, and I got really sick from it. I went from around 18 stone down to 13 stone and ended up having to move back to my mum's. As soon was back on my feet I started to go out more - just to meet somebody if I'm being honest. I was so sick of being lonely; I just missed my family so much. My ex had moved on by this point and I had more than one guy threaten me on nights out or over the phone because of her. The last one did it in a night club. He told me to keep away from them both and from my son, but I didn't give a fuck what anybody said. He was my son and I wasn't going to just forget about him: I wasn't going anywhere. The only contact I had to try and get access to Dennon was my solicitor. I had not seen him for over a year by this time, and it hurt so much as I had been there from the beginning. His mother wouldn't reply to any of the letters we sent her; she was making it as hard as possible for me to see him. I could not afford to keep doing all this - I just had to get myself sorted. Looking back now, I can kind of understand what she did, but then it just seemed a waste of time, and as though I had nothing going for me.

Chapter 4

Then one night I ended up meeting a girl on a night out in Burton. She was a girl one of my friends had gone to school with and I didn't think she was much to look at, but I just wanted the company. My brother had got me a bit of work, working away, so we would talk on the phone all the time, texting and ringing each other most days. We ended up getting together and we would go out most nights. I remember the first time I went to meet her for dinner. We sat outside Claire's Accessories, which was where she worked; she was not the best looking girl in the world and I just thought surely I could do better for myself than this. Thinking back about it I wished I had walked away then but I didn't - I was lonely and I just wanted the company, so I made do with what I had.

She had a twin sister that would come out with us all the time and I actually got on with her really well. I can remember one night she told me she had a thing for me and that I was with the wrong twin but I just made a joke of it, laughing and saying that it would never happen. Thinking about it now though, I think it would have been a smoother time if I had gone with her; the only thing that put me off was that she had slept around a lot. Most of the lads she had worked with had been with her and even my school friend told me he had slept with her. She was bad.

One night she called me to come pick her up from wherever she was, and she had just been with a married black man. (I only knew that because my friend told me who he was. He worked with the guy she had slept with and he told me a few days later.) As I got there she was tottering towards the car trying to pull her knickers back on. It was horrendous - the car reeked of sex. I think the family was just awful; they thought they were really something, but clearly had no morals.

After a few weeks dating this girl I found that she was going with a wrongen before me and it made me feel a bit sick and disgusted. I knew I could do better but I was stuck, as I didn't want to be on my own again.

I then got a job at a food factory call Kerry Foods. It was horrendous: I had to work night shifts and she would go out with her twin sister all the time; I didn't trust them one bit - how could I with their history? It was just mishap after mishap, the whole relationship. I caught her on her phone texting her ex behind my back and when I confronted her about it she said she was sorry and wouldn't do it again, but the little trust I had was gone. I should have just left her there and then, but I never - even though I knew I was silly to stay with her. We had moved into a little flat we got in a place called Winshill. It was not nice at all, it's a really rough part Burton, but it was cheap.

Her mum and dad weren't pleased about her getting

with me from the start. They hated tattoos and her mum was really stuck up; they really thought they were something. One day we had gone round to theirs and they were buying her younger sister a new car. They had £9,000 on the kitchen table to pay for it and her mum came over to me and said did I want to hold it, and have a feel of what it felt like to hold that amount of money. I replied with, "No its ok! I had already had double that amount when I was 18." Her face dropped and she walked away huffing at how rude I had been. My partner looked over at me and glared as if to say, why did you just say that! It didn't go down very well and she argued with me all the way home about it.

In their heads they thought because of how I looked and that I wasn't some lawyer or such that they could talk down to me all they liked, but I don't give a fuck who you think you are you don't talk to me like that!

***

I got a job at a local B&Q warehouse where the pay wasn't too bad, but the hours were long. She was still at university during that time, so I was paying for everything and helping towards her uni. She was only at Birmingham, so she would just go on the train the days that she was there.

Her mum was always giving her shit for being with me; she even called a couple of times to tell me what a scum-bag I was. She really was a nasty woman. Looking back on it now, I don't think her mum was mentally right in the head. She was only a secretary to one of the doctors at the local hospital but it made her have a really high opinion of herself; her partner worked at the local brewery, but the way they went on you would have thought they were millionaires. To be honest, I didn't mind her dad - he seemed ok - but I could not stand her mum, she was a right old witch. I think that's where my missus got it from, thinking about it. As time went on, being with her only got worse; we would split then get back together so many times. I just wanted to be with somebody who loved me - that's all anyone really wants, isn't it? She would drink most nights and it really got on my nerves how drunk she would get.

Meanwhile I had started to save some money so I could finally buy some professional tattooing machines. I had always tattooed but could never get hold of proper stuff for how expensive it was; it was so hard back then, as there was no internet or television shows making the industry as big as it is now. After making that first order I couldn't wait till it all came - I had spent £540 on a full kit from the tattoo factory. I went round to see Andy (the local shop), who I had been friends with for years, and he really helped me get started. The first person I tattooed was a bloke called Keg, who was my mum's boyfriend at the time. I did a Red Indian woman on his arm - it was not bad too. That was it! From then on I just wanted to tattoo all the time; if I wasn't at work I'd be tattooing. I did most of the lads I worked with and before I knew it word soon got out. I was so full of work that I could make £700 a week on top of my wages, and I kept buying more stuff to try and get better. My missus had soon left uni and her mum got her a job at the hospital she worked at.

Whenever we went out at the weekends, she would al-

This was when I was around 3 and a half at the house in Leeds.

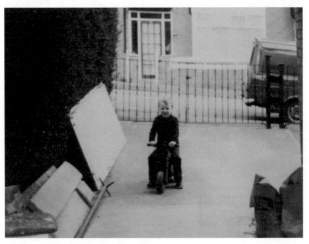

At 11 Landseer Grove in Leeds aged 4.

Aged 5 and a half with my puppy. My mum gave it away to a little girl that was really poorly.

The flat that we moved into when we first moved to Swadlincote from Leeds.

Sat with my mum aged 6. I was always a mummy's boy and sleep in her bed until I was 7.

About 7 years old. Tara thinks I look like Keith Chegwyn.

Christmas at Chiltern Road was always good.

Aged 10 this was just before I got into Bros.

On Holiday with my mum. This was when she had to cover my back with sanitary pads because I was so blistered from sunburn.

Like I said, such a camp child. This is actually rather horrifying. Ha!

Aged 15 with my Sister Lesley. I always used to look older than I was although now I look younger than I am so I guess it paid off.

My brother Mark, Auntie Tracey and some random bird at a party when we lived at Chiltern Road.

This was when I was 18 with my British Bulldog Ash.

Me with Dennon when he was few months old. Ash with Meg, Pig and Po on my legs. I am 21.

With Dennon when he was about 1.

Danni Filth at Bloodstock he is so little.

Kevin Paul Tattoo's.

This is when we were in Camden for New Year's when we first got together we stopped to take a photo by the lock it was a really nice frosty morning.

Tara & Rocco she had not long woken up from the operation. I was so glad that they were both fine after the drama.

Me with Rocco just after he was born.

Tara & Rocco aged about 3.

Tara & Rocco on San Diego Beach.

Dressed Rocco up as chicken when he was 4 months old.

A few months after we got back from our Vegas wedding. We had a party. Tara was 7 months pregnant.

In my scrubs just after Revan was born.

Tara just after haven Raven. She was happy to cuddle him straight after the birth unlike with Rocco.

This was when I took Rocco to go see his mum and new brother, he is kept saying 'no he didn't want him.'

Tara, me & Rocco on our official wedding day 4th January 2012 in Las Vegas. She was 5 months pregnant with Raven it was such a Hill Billy affair ha!

A rare family picture of all four of us together. Revan was only a few weeks old.

A Photo of Revan my wife took shows his attitude, such a cheeky boy.

Revan and I when he was about 18 months. (Photo by Jules)

Raven and I watching James Arthur rehears. The boys always came on tour with us when they were young.

ways disappear for half hour at a time then act really odd when she came back. It was obvious that she was up to something. After a while we ended up moving over to Derby for a fresh start and I ended up getting work in a local tattoo shop just helping out. The bloke that had the studio was a bit of a dick, but it was a start. It didn't take long before most of the clients wanted me, not him, to tattoo them; he didn't like it, and he started to give some bullshit about why he wanted me to leave. I looked at going to work with Andy, but the guy I had just left working with had told him he would not be happy if he set me on. Andy is such a soft guy that he just didn't want to upset anybody. Then I had a local guy offer to set me up a shop in Burton and I ended up doing it.

It was now 2006 and I was 28. As soon as the guy I worked for in the past found out about my studio he was not happy. I started to get death threats all the time and my windows kept getting put through. They were trying to make out it was a local gang doing it, so I contacted them direct. I asked them if they had a problem with me and they said if it was true they had a problem with me, then I would already be dead. I knew for sure now that it was down to the guy I worked for. After I told the gang that this guy was trying to make out that it was them doing the threats and damage they spent a little time putting him in line one night and he never came round me again. Everything was going good with work but my missus hated it; she was full of resentment about me being happy with my life. She would try to pull me down every chance she could get and over time it really started to drag me down. The thing is, when somebody is getting at you all the time you start to believe it; you start to believe that every word they're saying is true and that it's you and not them – it's a form of bullying. Deep down I knew she was a bully and had issues buried within her. She would get drunk most nights then start on me. She would start yelling and shouting obscene words and nasty remarks, and then it would turn into her trying to throw punches, plates and the likes at me, and on one occasion she even tried to glass me. I would have to try and pin her down, holding her hands away from me, and just wait for her to fall asleep. She would wake up the next day like nothing had happened. Every time she would enter the room I was in, I would get that cold feeling like I did as a kid when Phil was around. I hated her but she had made me feel that I could not live without her.

She hated me tattooing girls; every time I did she would accuse me of sleeping with them. She would go on my Facebook and Myspace and read everything, and she would block anything from a girl and delete them off my profiles; she wasn't right in the head. It had got to the point that I was scared of my phone going off around her just in case it was a female. The drinking was getting out of hand too; she would be downing two bottles of wine most nights. Sometimes she would leave a bottle of wine in the fridge half empty, so I would piss in it. That way I knew the next day I had one up on her when I was sat watching her drink it. Obviously I know now it was an awful thing to do, but back then my life was in a different place and it was the only thing I could think of to get her back slightly.

I ended up leaving the shop in Burton and got a studio in Derby. It was a lovely little place up a side street called Green Lane in the town centre. Two lesbians called Mel and Gemma Marmalade ran the shop; it was a little retro shop and sold everything from cups and straws to sex toys. They asked me if I wanted to rent half their premises, so that's what I did. It gave me a good start to building a reputation for my style of work in Derby.

***

Before long I had split with my missus again. My mum got sick of it happening, so she ended up giving me the money back I gave her years ago. I brought a little flat just outside Derby town centre which I paid for outright, and I had the little studio too. Things were looking up.

I still found it hard to talk to girls - I mean, I have always been shy but living with years of abuse makes you feel bad about yourself, and you have no confidence left. I ended up getting back with my ex because she kept texting and calling for weeks saying she was going to change and quit the drinking, so it was just easier than meeting new people. I've never really been keen on doing all those dating things when you first get with someone.

I started to make a lot of friends in the tattoo industry and was starting to work at most the conventions around the UK. Everything was going well apart from my missus started her usual games again, drinking and taking drugs.

She would get drunk at the after parties, and during

one party she kissed one of the other female artists. I was so ashamed - I dreaded what people must have been saying behind my back. She was always sneaking off and I knew she was doing this type of thing all the time.

The success of the shop meant I needed an assistant; he used to work at a shit studio down the road till he met me. He was a nice lad from a good family - a bit camp and not much to look at but he could draw, so I helped him get started properly. After a while he would go everywhere with me, and he started to see what my missus was like on a day to day basis. Everybody knew what she was like. It was at this point my mum helped me go back to court to get some access to see my son Dennon again, but after all this time with no contact she wouldn't reply to any of the letters at first. It was only after a lot of going back and forth I finally got to see him again.

I was so happy and my missus didn't like it at all- I was happy and she couldn't stand it. I started to spend a lot of time with two tattooists I know, Jason Butcher from Essex and Jo Harrison from Birmingham. Paul Booth, the guy I loved growing up, had tattooed Jason. He would tell me how he worked and what machines to use. It was fascinating listening to the stories and it was to become very useful, as it helped my work grow so much. Jo was really good at colour work. Between the both of them I picked up so much over the years, I owe them a lot still for what they did for me.

During one convention in Wales one year there was a party in one of the hotel rooms. I noticed my missus had disappeared to the toilet for around half hour and when she reappeared I saw she was with my assistant, I knew what they had been up too, but I just didn't care any more: I fucking hated her; she could have openly told me what she was doing and I still wouldn't have cared. The thing is with stuff like this, if you give people a little bit of space their true colours will show, and that's when you know what you're really dealing with. There are a lot of people who like to think they're having a laugh behind my back, but trust me they are not. I know about everything that goes on, and just because I don't react on first instance doesn't mean I haven't registered what has happened.

***

In December 2008 I decided to go on a trip to New York. She kept saying we should get married and I really didn't want to, but I thought since I couldn't get rid of her maybe if we got married she would stop the drinking and drug taking at shows. So I went along with it. Over the last month or so I had been feeling really low from the stress of being with her. I was getting that panic feeling coming back again but I daren't tell her about it as I was afraid she'd see it as a sign of weakness - if she even cared. I had been to the doctor's the week before we went to get some antidepressants, and I even started drinking vodka to help keep me chilled the day of the flight, I was so anguished. I just really hated my life at this point.

We never really talked the whole time we were there. It was New Year's Eve and the day of the wedding, which we had booked to do in Central Park. You would think it would have been really romantic but there was no love, not even a kiss. The moment it was over we went back to the hotel to get changed. We didn't really talk much or show any form of happiness about the fact we were just married. That night we got in bed and just turned our backs on each other. I lay there thinking how it was the end of 2008 and I had turned 30 that year, and just remember feeling my utter lowest. I was thinking, I'm 30 years old and I've got hardly anything to show for it. I really just wanted to end my life - it was just a waste of time. Meeting her was the biggest mistake I had ever made.

When we got back home she said she wanted us to buy a house together, something nice so we could have kids and raise them there. She knew how much I always wanted more kids, so I jumped at the idea. I put the flat up for sale and when it had sold used the money towards the house that she wanted to buy. She said my name would not be able to go on the mortgage for some reason, and I just agreed with her. I spent the best part of £30,000 if not more on doing the house out, knocking it all through and almost starting from scratch with it all. It looked amazing once it was done. Then she asked if I would lend her the money for a new car she wanted - some fancy two-seater thing - and I gave her about £12,000 for that. That was it: it pretty much wiped me out of all the money from the sale of the flat. It wasn't long after that she started with her games again, getting drunk and taking drugs on nights out. Yet again I caught her in our bathroom with my mate's girlfriend, kissing each other. She repulsed me.

***

A few weeks later I had a visit from a local landlord. I knew him from around town and he asked me to pop up his place one day for a chat I knew he was involved in gang stuff but he seemed a nice guy. When I got there he asked me to go upstairs with him, and I was on my guard by this point, just in case I was being set up. When I went in there were 3 big nasty-ass dogs walking around; one of them kept sniffing around my balls - it would not fuck off. He said he had a phone call recorded that he wanted me to hear and my heart was pounding wondering what the hell he was going to let me listen to, but it turned out it was from Charles Bronson; he was the guy who had spent over 30 years in prison - for stealing £27 from a post office I believe it was .He has got really big and well known for costing the government more money than any other prisoner in the UK. He would take people hostage, or just smash up the prison, I got told he once had two people hostage and his demands to let them go were a cheese and pickle sandwich, a cup of tea and a helicopter. They even made a film about him with Tom Hardy in the role of Bronson.

The landlord played the phone call recording, and I can't repeat what he said but Bronson was going to send me some stuff for the studio. I didn't think much of it at first. I get a lot of people saying they have stuff for me, but not many ever come through, so I just forgot about it. Then within two days I got a thing in the post from the prison, all stamped up and addressed to me. I ripped open the envelope and there inside was a drawing that Bronson had done of himself in his cell. It was really well done - I've got it framed and put it in the studio. In with the picture he also sent me a cd of him in his cell just talking about how he feels and about his days in there, a little bit like a diary. I popped the cd on to have a listen, and it was so bizarre! He was talking about taking a sausage that he got for dinner for a walk to his cell on a piece of string. When the other inmates asked him what he was doing he said he was taking his sausage dog for a walk. It was one of the oddest things I had ever heard, but he seemed a nice guy all the same. He still sends me Xmas cards and bits every so often.

***

It was now coming up to the summer of 2009 and I got asked to work a rock festival by a client I had. They asked me if I would set up a mini studio backstage and they would ask the acts if they wanted to get tattooed. I agreed - I thought it would be an awesome thing to do. I went along and I ended up tattooing the lead singer of Cradle of Filth, Danni Filth. He was a nice guy and he asked for the Wolfman from the classic 50s film. It was really cool for me because Paul Booth had tattooed him. I became good friends with him and he would come up to the studio every now and then.

I spent most of the day at the festival with a guy who looked a bit like Bon Jovi, but I didn't have a clue who he was. At the end of the night everybody was waiting for the main event to come up, a band called Europe. They did a song everyone knows called the Final Countdown, and it turned out the guy I was with all day was their lead singer. I couldn't believe it - I would have given him so much more time if I'd known! It was amazing to see them live, and when they played that song it went down so well.

The girl who ran the festival texted me a lot after that. We got on really well and we would talk most days; in fact I could not wait to wake up the next morning to get away from my missus so I could text her. I never did anything with her but she made me feel good about myself for the first time in ages.

Then one day it was around October time and my wife came in from work and said she was leaving. I was shocked but the only thing I could think about was the girl I met at the festival. As soon as she left I texted her and told her and it turned out she was in the same place as me - her fella was not good to her. He was a fat, ugly ginger guy and she didn't feel anything for him; she had just been with him a long time.

We started to see each other as much as we could but I made it clear I was not going to do anything until she was single – I'd had that done to me, and I didn't think it was fair to her boyfriend. She kept saying she was going to tell him, but never did, and this went on for about 4 weeks. It always felt a bit odd with her anyway: she was more like a good friend or a cool auntie - she was the same age as me but felt so much older; thinking about it now, I wish we'd just kept it as friends now - so I decided to go out one Thursday night with some friends and I'm not sure why, but we ended up in one of those really tacky bars that I wouldn't normally go in. It was a laugh though, and we were stood by the bar when this pair of girls came down some stairs, laughing. They started talking to my friend about his tattoos and then started talking to us all. They were only young, and one of them was a pretty, short girl; she had long dark hair and she said her name was Tara. She was so pretty! We were speaking for hours and we got on really well. She would talk about the most pointless things, but I was just happy to just sit and watch her talking – admittedly, rarely taking in what she was saying for just looking at her. After being around bitter people all the time it was a refreshing change to be with someone so nice and carefree. We exchanged numbers and I had a smile on my face once again.

The next day we were texting each other all day and agreed to meet up that night in town. We were having drinks together when she told me she'd had a falling out with her parents and was stopping between two friends' houses. I told her to come back to mine, and we just sat on the sofa talking about what we both wanted out of life. Tara said all she wanted was to make someone happy and to have children with them; raise them in a loving home and grow old together, which is all I ever wanted too. It was so nice to spend time with somebody whose life was so simple and wasn't bitter at all. She was only 19. The next day I told her to go and get some new clothes from town, as she didn't have much with her at the time. When I finished work she met me and we went back home and ordered a take away and watched the X-Factor. I told her that she was more than welcome to stay at mine until she could sort herself out, but in fact we never left each other's side from that point on! It's crazy to think that I met her on the Thursday night and she was living with me come the Sunday, but it just felt right; something between us just clicked into place.

***

We had our first Christmas together and things were going really well. Tara told me she had never been to London, so I decided to take her away for New Year's Eve. We stayed in a nice penthouse in Camden, overlooking the lock and the market. We went out and explored around the market, did the London Eye and then went back to the hotel to freshen up before going out for the night to see in the start of a New Year together. We went to this bar in Camden and had a few drinks, but then she started complaining she had pains in her stomach, I thought she was overreacting about nothing: little did I know it would eventually turn out to be something quite bad. The next day we took a photo on the lock before getting the train home and we had planned to go round her mum and dad's so they could meet me for the first time.

We got there around 5pm on New Year's Day. It was such an entertaining night too! They had a group of friends round and were still celebrating New Year, so they were still drunk. I will never forget her mum dancing on a chair, then falling off and smashing a pot with her head, her arm knocking her drink everywhere - including all over her friend's new partner - and she just jumped back up, got another drink and carried on dancing. They were just an ordinary, hardworking family and it was so nice to be around that after my ex's stuck up lot.

***

The next week we found out Tara was pregnant. We

had only been together around 10 weeks but I was so happy about it. A week or so later though, she was still getting pains in her stomach and side - the same as in London. We went to the doctor's and they said they weren't sure, so sent her to the hospital straight away. I was so scared they were going to say she was losing the baby but it turned out she had a grumbling appendix. She had to stay in hospital for around a week. They offered her either an operation if the pains didn't go, or some tablets. Of course, she could have lost the baby, but luckily she was ok and the pains subsided with some tablets.

I tried to get divorced as soon as possible and I made my wife a really good offer but she wouldn't take it: she said she wanted it all. This went on for months because she wanted to drag it out and make things as hard as possible for me. She just couldn't stand the idea that I was moving on with my life and was happy for once. She was just a bitter person. All my money was tied up in the house and she knew it. I was forced into having to get credit cards to try keep on top of everything. I had also found out that my ex had allegedly moved in with somebody else, and it turned out that she was supposedly cheating on me with him for over 6 months before she left. I didn't care: I just wanted out of the marriage and her out of my new life and to never have anything to do with her again.

After about 4 months I had to go to mediation, since she wouldn't make an agreement with the solicitors. But all she wanted was to get me in a room so she could twist everything. She just wanted to talk to me, not sort anything with the house at all, and it ended up getting us nowhere. All I wanted was to make a fresh start with Tara and my new family, but it got dragged on for almost 2 years before it finally got sorted. I ended up having to sell my shop for a loss and got in to loads of debt.

After all the messing about she'd done, the money I got back out the house didn't even cover it all. I was back to square one, renting places and working for other people. The good thing was, at last I was with someone who made me happy and that I actually felt loved for once. She was still bitter about the split - I think that was why she made everything so hard.

***

I remember it was the day before we had the baby when my divorce came through. It was like life was falling into place all over again, and for good for once! Rocco Jack was born, and he was the best thing ever to happen to me - I loved him so much from the second he was born! It was a difficult labour and birth, though. Tara had got to 39 weeks and they said he was going to be about 10lbs, so they gave her a sweep to try and bring him on before she could get to a further 3 weeks along. That was on the Thursday; the next day about 11 that night her contractions started and we went to hospital, but they said she was only 1cm dilated and to go home and wait it out until she was at a point to push. This happened on and off for a week: every night the little monkey would give his mummy the worst contractions from 11pm until the early hours, but every time we got to hospital they would say she was only 1 or 2cms. Then on the following Friday we went in just before midnight and they finally said she was 4cms and it was happening, it was horrible seeing her in pain until she had an epidural.

After a few hours the doctors came in and said he wasn't getting enough oxygen to his brain and they had to take blood from him while he was still inside. Eventually it got to a point where she could push and he just wouldn't come out. I remember the midwife saying she could see his face, but they were still trying to get her to push. After about half hour they took her for some suction thing to help her push him out but he still wouldn't budge. Eventually the surgeon came over and asked why she hadn't been c-sectioned ages ago. As they started to cut and bring him out Tara was complaining she could feel everything happening, and as I looked over to the surgeon I could see Rocco all floppy in the midwife's arms. I turned back to try and shield Tara from seeing him, as she was already panicking about the pain. At that point she asked to be put under because she was sure her epidural was wearing off, and I was rushed out of the room not knowing fully why she was being put to sleep or if my baby boy was breathing or not. After just over 4 minutes a midwife came out with Rocco: he was fine and I got to hold him! I think that's why he prefers me to his mum at bedtime - because I was the first one to hold him and bond with him.

After an hour they had brought Tara round and she finally got to meet her son. As it turned out, the surgeon told us that if she had delivered him naturally she would have broken his neck and that the midwife had made an error in not asking for a C section to be done

– she had nearly cost us our son's life. It was horrible to hear but such a relief to know the surgeon came in at the right time. We were told that because she had tried to push him out and then they had to push him back in to pull him out of the C section cut, he had been shocked into not breathing. It was lucky he hadn't suffered any permanent damage. From that time on I knew I had to do all I could to provide for my new son. I had missed out on so many years with my first son, all the milestones and firsts. I didn't want this to happen again. I knew I was never going to make back the money I'd lost from the house or have the money to buy my own house again - at least for a good few years or more. From the second Rocco was born something in me changed. It was not all about me anymore. I did everything I could for him and I knew I had to do something more for my family.

Chapter 5

There was a TV show on at the time called London Ink. The main tattooist on the show had made himself quite well known all because he had tattooed David Beckham and was now charging silly amounts of money. So I thought if maybe I started to tattoo celebrities I might be able to charge a bit more and get on a TV show myself.

I tried every way possible to contact acts, and even tried contacting managements, agents, and anyone that had a link to people. Nothing worked and after about 6 months I was starting to give up hope. Then one night we were watching a TV show about N-dubz and it showed Dappy getting tattooed. It was shit! I knew I could've done it a lot better. I had one last go at trying to make contact with them, thinking they could be my big break, but sadly I got nowhere. I finally got rid of the last string that was tying me down to my ex-wife, and Tara and our new baby and I could finally set up our own life in our own home. While we were arranging funds, though, we ended up having to move in with my mum for a while to get ourselves sorted.

***

I never got anything back from any of the acts, so had almost given up hope. I'd finally had enough working for other people and wanted to find myself a private studio, so I had gone to view this little two- storey building on Great Northern Road. It was too expensive though, and didn't really have a good feeling about it - like it wasn't for me. I'd gone back to my car and noticed this bright orange building with CROW written on the front of it, and there was a sign on the front saying Unit to Let. I contacted the number on the board and asked to view it. The landlord was called Dale and he told me that he was a carpenter and he created artistic wood pieces; the rest of his tenants were photographers and such - all from artistic backgrounds. There was even a gay guy in there that made little pottery knobs and penis shaped hooks. I decided to take it: they were all from the same kind of industry as me - all arty and hard-working.

The unit was coming on really well and the clients were slowly building up again, then one day at work I had an old friend called Andy Meakin, who used to run some night clubs in Burton back in the day, come into the studio to get some tattoo work done. He was telling me he now worked for Loughborough Uni and that he got lots of big music acts come down to play gigs for the Freshers' Fayre and Christmas balls. I told him to let me know if any of them ever wanted to get inked, and he said that he had Gym Class Heroes in in two weeks' time, which I thought was perfect as the lead singer was Travie McCoy and he was covered in ink.

About a week went by and I didn't hear anything back. I was starting to think I wouldn't get him, but one day they called me to say that Travie did want to get inked; they sent me their management details and we started to talk about it all and arrange for when it would happen. I couldn't wait to meet him - I thought this would be the break I needed - but the day before the meeting was due I heard on the radio that Travie had been rushed to hospital with a stomach infection. When I found out it was true and the gig had been pulled I was gutted, but they told me to go down anyway. When I got there they had found a replacement in Dynamo the Magician who was doing a meet and greet with the students instead of there being a gig. I had Tara and my Dennon with me and we went up to meet him in his dressing room, and Dennon told him he watched all his TV shows. He did some magic tricks for us and it was mesmerizing how he did some of them. Tara was in tears with laughing from shock! He asked for my card and said he wanted to get more ink, and the people at the uni asked if I would go back the following week, as they had more acts they wanted me to meet.

Rocco was now 1 year old and we had just found out we were expecting another baby. I couldn't wait to be a father again! I went back on the Tuesday night and a new band called Rizzle Kicks was playing. They had just had their first hit single come out - Down with the Trumpets. It was a catchy song and had got quite good reviews on the radio. I watched the gig from backstage and they were really good. The band was told that I was there and they wanted a meet, so we went back to their dressing room after the show. They were really nice, polite guys and said they wanted lots of new stuff tattooed. They took a card and said they would contact me soon. I didn't think they would, but about a week or two later Harley from the band called me and said that he wanted to come up to start a sleeve. This was it - my big break!

He came up with the bassist from the band and they both wanted to get some script done. It wasn't my normal type of stuff but I didn't really care. I just wanted to get my first celeb. Harley wanted it done like the script on their album, which made it look like a 5 year old had drawn it. I knew I could do so much better, but at the end of the day that's how he wanted it so that's how I did it. He loved it and said he wanted more. He offered to pay me for it, but I said I didn't want the money – just to get my name out there with all the other acts he came into contact with, and just for him to spread the word about me. As a result, he tweeted about coming up and it sent my twitter up by about 500 followers by the end of the day.

***

About a week later I got a call from a guy who said he was the drummer to Tinie Tempah. Tinie was going really well at that time and had worked with some amazingly top people, so I jumped at working with him, I was thinking of all the people it could eventually lead to next. When I met him he was not what I was expecting; he was a little short guy who lived with his mum. He gave me the big talk about all the people he had worked with, so I had to take him on his word, and he had photos with everybody from Will Smith to

Justin Bieber. I tattooed him in London about a week or two later and asked him to do the same as Harley - get my name out there! The word was already out by now, and my local paper the Derby Telegraph had run a story on me starting to tattoo celebrities, which started to help build even more trade in the studio and with the acts, and Tinie's drummer kid stood by his promise and started to spread the word about me.

As well as my little tattoo studio in Derby I ended up getting a job working twice a week for a tattooist called Lal Hardy, who owns New Wave Tattoo in Muswell Hill, North London. I have big respect for him: he was one of the first tattooists around in London in the 70s, and he had tattooed a lot of stars over the years. I thought I might learn a thing or two from him about his time in the trade. Lal was also pretty good friends with Paul Booth and I loved to hear some of the stories about his time with him. I remembered seeing a thing about Paul Booth in a magazine called Skindeep that was done at Lal's shop, and now I was working there! It was so cool finally to be doing what I always wanted to do somewhere where I never thought I would ever be working.

I then had a call from an actor called Paddy Considine. He said he was looking to get a portrait done of his dad's favourite actor, Lee Marvin. He came in about a week later and seemed like such a nice guy. He kept himself to himself, and I don't know why but I was so nervous about tattooing him. I was a big fan of some of the films he had been in, like *America* and *Dead Man's Shoes*. He was so cool and not full of himself at all; I really liked that about him. The tattoo ended up taking me a lot longer than it would normally but I just wanted to get it 100% perfect and right. He seemed really happy with it and I stayed in touch with him afterwards. He even brought me a poster from two of his films to put up in the studio. They are so cool! One of them, (limited to 50 prints I think he said) is from his film *Tyrannosaur* and the other one from *Dead Man's Shoes,* and he signed it with a lovely personal message for me.

***

It was now November 2011. Rocco was coming up for 15 months and I said to Tara that I would take her away for the first weekend of December, as we hadn't really had much time for just the two of us since Rocco was born. I told her we were going to Ireland and she was really excited, as she had hardly ever travelled before. The fact was that I had actually booked for us both to go to New York and was going to surprise her at the airport, but as impatient as she is she kept asking a tonne of questions. What would the weather be like? What was the place called? How were we getting there? And what baby shops did they have in Ireland, as she was looking for things for the new baby?

I couldn't keep it secret any more and told her she could either find out now or wait, but of course she needed to know there and then. When I told her she squealed with excitement - I loved seeing her so happy and excited! We left Rocco with my mum, and my dad came down to help her. We went down to London to catch our flight, both of us looking forward to exploring NY City and shopping for the kids. I treated this like it was my first time in New York since I didn't really have fond memories of the first time I was out there. We really enjoyed ourselves and before long it was time to come home.

***

When we got back we found a little rented house in Derby. It was perfect for the time being, as it was just a few doors up from Tara's parents and they could help as much as possible with Rocco and eventually the new baby, since I was going back and forward to London a lot of the time. We had been back a week and half, and knew we wanted to go over to the States again. We talked about going to the West Coast via Las Vegas, so we booked 2 weeks away before what I hoped would be a bumper packed work year. We enjoyed Christmas as a family and on the 29th December 2011 found out Tara was expecting another boy. I couldn't believe it - 3 boys - I was so happy!

We packed our bags and on New Year's Day headed down to London again for our flight to Las Vegas. It was Rocco's first time on an aeroplane, and we were really surprised by how well behaved he was. The Virgin stewardesses made the flight loads more bearable, though! Rocco came off the plane with bright red lipstick all over his face where he had been walking up the aisles and they kept scooping him up and kissing him.

We had booked 3 nights in Las Vegas and then arranged to pick up an RV and drive from Vegas to Los Angeles. When we got there it seemed like a really nice place - not as mad as you would think. That night when we got back to the hotel we started talking about getting married. We had mentioned it before back home so it wasn't just an out of the blue thing, but we thought while we were out in Vegas why not do it there. Tara rang her dad and asked if they would mind if we did it without any family being there and they said to go for it, as it would be cheap and it would be good to start married life with no debt, unlike some weddings that cost people thousands of pounds.

So the next day we went down to the little white wedding chapel and asked them what we would need to do. They told us to head to the Clark County Marriage Bureau to obtain a marriage licence. We had to walk the whole length of the Strip to get there and even past the famous pawn shop on the way. Once we had got the licence we went back to the chapel and booked the wedding for the morning. We arranged for a limo to pick us up from our hotel and take us to the chapel, and told them we would need to hire a dress. When it was all booked it had cost us $500, which worked out at about £350 - an absolute bargain. It may not be the fancy magazine, stately home inspired wedding, but it would be *our* wedding! Tara went off to choose a dress and I bought a tuxedo printed T shirt for $10. It was all so cheap and hillbilly it looked like something Britney Spears would have done when she was having a meltdown!

The limo picked us up and took us to the chapel. It was so different from my first wedding: I actually love Tara and I wanted to marry her for love not for the sake of it, like with my ex-wife. When Tara walked down the aisle I was stood there with Rocco next to me in his pushchair and it was all over and done with in about half hour, including the photographs being taken. The next morning was our last in Vegas and we went for breakfast and then headed to go pick up the RV; little did I know the vacation was going to turn from that point on. The company that we were hiring the RV from made us pay out more than we we'd been told by the travel agents. I had to go and set up a credit card because they didn't accept cash and then when we finally got on the road we had to go to the nearest gas station to fill up and stock up on food from Walmarts. We finally got on the road to Arizona and it was at that point that I really understood how big America was. Until you are there and you're driving for hours it doesn't really hit you.

We had been on the road now for a long time and it was getting dark; with every hour that passed the more deserted the place was getting. It was coming up to 11 at night and it was beginning to creep us out; we were in the middle of the desert - pitch black - so we decided to pull in to the first motel we found and it was like something from a horror film. In fact Tara said it reminded her of a film called *Vacancy.* The lights were flickering, a head popped from round the corner of one of the doors and then closed it again, I turned around as fast as I could and we finally found somewhere else about an hour and a half later.

We got the room keys and tried to get some sleep before setting off again in the morning, which was not easy to do since the bathroom window would not close, and I just kept thinking about all sorts of horrible things happening. The next morning at about 6am we handed in the keys and set back off on our trip. It wasn't until then we realised that we had somehow ended up on Route 66. It was an absolutely beautiful morning: the sun was just rising and I was just glad we hadn't been killed in our sleep.

We were heading now towards San Diego. It took us a while, but we got there in the end. We found a little trailer park which was just on the beach front and we ended up staying there for around 3 days. It was lovely waking up every morning to the waves crashing on the sand. We soon got bored with it though, as due to the season there wasn't much to do, so we packed up and headed on down to LA.

When we got there about dinner time the first thing we did was go down to Venice Beach, which was not as good as I thought it would be. Then we headed on over to Santa Monica Pier. Rocco loved this bit, as it was full of rides and fairground attractions. I'd had about my lot of the West Coast by this point! We then went on up to Beverley Hills. It was so run down and not what I thought it would be at all. We couldn't find anywhere to park this fucking motor home. I ended up finding a cheap motel just so we could freshen up, since the shower in the RV was cold water that came out like a piss trickle and barely did the job between the three of us.

As we were walking into the room I saw a hooker going into the room next to us with this posh old guy. It was shocking, and when I turned on the TV most of the channels were just porn. I went out to the truck to get some bits and there were some gang members hanging around outside. They kept coming over to talk to me and I think that was the last straw. I just said, let's go home. It was about a week before we were due back, but I had seen all the LA I wanted to and so we packed up and made our way to the airport. I gave them some bullshit about a water leak back at home and we got lucky and managed to get on a flight home that night. It was so nice to land back in the UK. Whenever I see motorhomes now I still want to burn every one of the evil things!

Chapter 6

About 3 days after we got home I had a call from a guy called Derry in a band called the Risk, which was on the X- Factor. I told him to come up, and to send any artwork he wanted. This was really good news, as at the time the show had just ended and they were about to start the X-Factor live tour with the rest of the band and the winners, Little Mix. Derry came up to the studio that week and we worked on him till about 2 in the morning; this did a lot for Twitter again and got me back in the press. I was working 7 days a week trying to keep the studio open, as well as pushing all the celeb things that I was trying to do.

Meanwhile, I had developed a real bad chest infection, which started while we were away in America. I'd had it around 4 weeks now, so I decided to go to the doctor's about it and they sent me for a chest X ray about 3 weeks later. When it's things like your chest and having an infection that just won't go, you worry in case it's something serious. I was panicking it could be cancer and they would give me bad news; I'd heard so many stories from clients who had lost people to cancer and I kept thinking, what if I had it? I might not see my little boy being born, or see both my sons grow up. It really hurt to think about it - I wanted to be there for them so much. If anything ever happened to me, Tara would be on her own with the boys. I was so scared of what the outcome would be - it was one of the most frightening times of my life.

I had a young lad come into the shop who'd lost his dad when he was young: he went off the rails and ended up on drugs and going to prison. I hated the thought of this happening to my boys. It was about 3 weeks before I got the ok, and I was so relieved to hear the good news! I still worry now about getting cancer, or my boys getting anything wrong with them: when you have kids they become your whole life. All this celebrity work started because of them - to keep them safe and healthy; to give them everything I never had, and to keep them from the life I turned to when I was younger. They are my whole world, and from the second I wake up till I go to sleep I worry about them.

Then there was the girl who came in once with a portrait of her little baby boy; he was only about 2 weeks old in the photo I tattooed from. I asked her if this was an old photo, and she told me that it was the last one she ever took of him before he died. I was so shocked I went cold. She told me that he died in her arms; he just went really limp and she knew he was gone. It really upset me to hear what she had gone through; if anything like that happened to my boys it would kill me. I felt so sorry for her - she was only about 19. Things like this just make me worry about my boys all the time: I don't know how I would cope with it happening to me.

***

By now the drummer lad that I'd tattooed before was telling anybody with a music link about me, and I was getting every dick out there trying to get a cheap tattoo. I had to put a stop on who came up, as it was getting out of hand, but at the same time I wanted to show respect for the help they had given me. Derry asked me to go tattoo him on the X Factor tour, and this was really cool; I was thinking that if the press would run a story about me doing it, then it would be very good for business.

I went to meet them at their hotel in Nottingham; it was insane - there were so many fans outside waiting already! How they knew where they were stopping was crazy. When the tour bus pulled up I had to get rushed in with the acts, and I saw everybody that I'd seen on the TV only weeks before. We did some bits on Derry there, and then took him to the venue later on. Me and Tara got to hang out back stage and we met them all except Little Mix, since they were the busiest of the acts. Marcus Collins said he wanted to come down soon, which was really cool as he was one of the most talented people on that year's show. Things were starting to pay off.

***

The lads from Rizzle Kicks called again asking if I could go down to them - they both wanted to get inked this time round. I got all their artwork printed off to take and popped down a week later with Tara, who was now about 7 months pregnant with our second son. When we got there it was not the type of place you would think someone in the music industry would live. It was down a little side street; a big 4 bedroomed student house they shared with some friends from back home. Their kitchen was a mess - take away tubs on the side, empty pop bottles and cans and bottles of beer everywhere. Tara had to give it a clean before I could start working. They were still within their first year of success so the 'glamour' had not yet filtered down to them. They were lovely guys. They've done a lot to help me and get my name out there, so I have big respect for them for doing that. After I had done both their tattoos I told them I would let them tattoo my leg. They didn't do an amazing job, but it was more about the memory of that moment and to show them I respected their help. They told me they'd given my number to Ed Sheeran after the first time I'd tattooed Harley, but I said I hadn't heard anything from him yet.

The next day while I was at work I had a phone call from a guy from Warner Brother Records called Luke Williams asking if I would tattoo him and an act he was working with. This seemed like a good idea and I was starting to build up some good contacts. He asked me if I would go on the Mobo Award gig with them, so I went down to the Birmingham event. It was all a bit too much for me, with all those gangster-like rappers talking street lingo. It made no sense to me.

I had a small room to work in and everybody wanted to come in to see what was going on. Nothing ever really came of the act, but Luke was really cool and I kept in touch with him after. I left the gig about 2 in the morning and I was fucked. It was all really stressful stuff. Everybody who was looking into what I was doing thought it was all really cool, fun stuff, but in reality it wasn't and I was missing so much of my little boy growing up, or spending time with my wife.

**

After about 4 weeks I got a text message saying, "Hi, this is Sheeza! This is my new number". I didn't have a clue who it was, and when I asked him he said, "It's Ed". I wondered at this point if it was Ed Sheeran, but didn't want to say anything in case it wasn't, so I asked "Ed who?" "Ed Sheeran," he said. "Who's this?" I told him who I was and he said he'd thought it was Kev from his management team, but as it happened he did want to get a tattoo at some point. He asked if I would come down next week. He seemed such a really nice guy on the phone so I went down to meet him.

He lived in a flat just down a side street - not where I thought he would live at all. He wasn't there yet when I arrived, so one of his friends let me in; they were ever so nice too and I set up ready for when he got back. His flat was full of awards and Lego and loads of stuff from his childhood. I could see he was close to it all still. When he arrived he seemed a bit shy at first, but he soon opened up and I got on with him so well from the start. I just felt comfortable around him, like I could just be myself. He had a painting tattooed that his dad loved - Starry Night by van Gogh. You could tell from the start he was really close to his family by the way he spoke about them all, it was nice to see. After I tattooed him I got him to tattoo me. He did a little guitar on my leg and signed it. It fucking hurt like hell!

After tattooing Ed I got lots of press wanting to do a story. I really didn't want for him to think I was selling him out because I really did like the guy, and the only way I was going to get more acts was if they could trust me. But I needed the press to let people know about what I was doing and so I would ask every act before I left what they would be happy with me saying if the press did call, and I have always stuck by that.

***

When I went back to London a couple of days later we had a meeting with a production company about doing a TV show about my life: it was basically a reality show about me. A year ago I would've jumped at the chance, but now I'd already had press coming out my ears and I was seeing that lots of young people were looking up to me so I wanted to do something more positive with my so-called fame. I had been thinking about everything that had happened to me in life so far, and the more I thought about it the more I came to believe in karma's rule. Everything I had ever profited from when I would steal as a kid, or any of the other stuff I use to do always ended up back-firing on me, or costing me much more in the long run. I didn't want anything bad to ever happen to my family, so from that point on everything I ever do is by the karma rule. Good things happen to good people.

Ed asked if I would pop back round his London flat again because there were some little bits he wanted to get done, one of them being his friend's logo because he was one of the guys who looked after him when he was poor. So we did that, then we started to just fill in some bits on his sleeve that needed finishing. Ed kept saying about how he wanted to try and get Mike Skinner from the Streets to write some lyrics for him and to get tattooed. Ed's manager said he was sure that he knew somebody who knew him and about ten minutes later he came back in with an email address for him. Ed dropped him an email and we got a reply in minutes saying he would pop round within the hour. It was so random, but every time I was round Ed's now something like this would happen. Mike turned up and he seemed like such a nice chap. He asked if he could video the whole thing and it ended up being a really long drawn out day, but we eventually finished around 7pm. Whenever I went round Ed's we ended up getting a Nando's, so we had ordered food before I left to go back home to Tara and Rocco.

***

The next day was the day the C section was booked for. We got to the hospital at 7:30 in the morning and had to wait till 11 for our scheduled slot. It's funny how they do them one in one out! Tara was panicking about it all as her head was focusing on what had happened last time, but the surgeon said it would be calmer this time as baby wasn't under any stress. They gave her a spinal again and then started to cut her open, and she was really relaxed, just talking to me about how much we thought he would weigh. Then we realised it was taking longer than usual, and I could hear the surgeon say something about turning the uterus as it was going to be difficult, I started to panic again, thinking and hoping he would be ok, and then I heard a massive cry and I sighed with relief. I looked over at Tara and she was tearing up. She'd missed all this the first time round and she was just saying "That's my baby - I can hear him crying!" It choked me up a bit.

He weighed less than his brother but he was fine and healthy; we called him Revan Ace. Tara, though, was told she couldn't have more kids without it being a risk to her health. The surgeon came in after she'd been stitched up and had relaxed for a while and explained the reason it had taken longer than usual was because her bladder was fused to her uterus by her first C-section's scar tissue. Any further pregnancies could lead to either the bladder or uterus rupturing, which would mean she would need more surgery.

Revan was an ugly little fella when he was born, but I loved him so much. I had to look after Rocco on my own for 3 days while Tara was in hospital, and I knew that even when she came out it would be really stressful, as she wouldn't be able to do anything for a while. Also I had to go back to work soon after to keep the bills paid. Her mum would come around and help as much as possible and my sister would help too. In the papers my career looked so glamorous but it really wasn't at all - it was long days from home back and forwards from London. Everybody thought my missus had a great life style, but all she was doing was stay at home with the kids on her own. She lost so many friends from it all too because people were jealous of the life they thought she had.

Around this time I found myself getting more and more into Karma - I'm a little OCD about things like that. One night we found a really old shitty Nokia phone in the back of a taxi; Tara asked me what we should do with it, and I said let's hand it in to the driver. I know he more than likely would have kept it but it was the right thing for us to do. A few days later we were in London and we had booked a cab to take us from the hotel to a theatre show. We were running late and rushing around and when I got out of the cab I realised I had lost my phone. The taxi had already pulled off and there was nothing I could do. We watched the show and when we went back to the hotel, we asked at Reception if it had been handed in, but it hadn't. The next morning when we checked out they said my phone had been found and to go pick it up from the taxi rank. I believe this was showing me that if we had kept the phone we found a few days earlier, then I wouldn't have got mine back. This was really important to me: it makes me believe that Karma really does work.

This is why I always try now to do only the right things in life and help people wherever I can. I would hate for me to do something wrong and Karma come back on my wife or kids. I wouldn't be able to live with myself.

Chapter 7

After a few weeks back at work I got a call from Frankie Cocozza, the first person to get kicked off the X Factor for openly saying he took drugs while on the show. He ended up with a big following from it all, and even went on Celebrity Big Brother. He was a nice young lad, but he was fucking nuts! When I met him he told me all about his time on the show and all the stuff after it. It wasn't all ups for him, he had a lot of abuse from the public after it all and he had blown all the money that he made. No one gives you help on how to deal with the fame you get, or warns you about how the big money soon stops after the show finishes. When you do shows like that they don't give you any financial help at all, or get you ready for what's about to happen to you. Soon as that ends, for most of them so does the fame. The more time I spent around the entertainment industry the more I started to realise it was a sad place to be, and I didn't really like it.

About a week later Ed called again and asked if I could go back down to see him; he said he had just bought a house in the countryside. I got ready what he wanted and took my two apprentices with me as well. It was so nice where he lived. It was deep in the countryside - you couldn't see anything for miles other than trees. All his friends were there and it was nice to meet such polite, nice people. My upbringing had been nothing like that at all. Nobody cared about who he was at all - he was just normal old Ed that they all went to school with. He had this rapper there called Big Nasty, who was walking around with no top on and cooked us a Jamaican stew. It was nice to see Ed just being himself, and I loved the house - it was so big inside, just what I wanted for my boys to grow up in. I knew after that I had to move to the countryside: that was my new goal. All I ever wanted now was a good life for the boys, and after seeing how Ed and all his mates turned out from living where they did I wanted the same for my boys.

***

I got an email from a guy who worked for a PA agency; he looked after some big names and he asked if I would go down to meet him, so I looked him up on the internet and saw he really did have some good names under him at the time. When I went down I tattooed him I found he was a lovely guy. He told me he could get me some more acts to tattoo and he was true to his word because a week or so later I had a meeting with Aiden Grimshaw at his office. He seemed a little bit over confident for the career he had, and was even a little bit rude at times. He had an album coming out, and to be fair to him it was really good - I still play it now. The only downfall was he didn't have much money behind him to get it to pay off. After I'd done his tattoo I went back to the hotel with my family and met up with a lad called Dru Wakely off a TV show called the Midnight Beast, which was also the name of his band. We talked about him wanting to start a sleeve and that he had seen my work online and was really up for me doing his tattoos. He said he would come down when he got a break from filming and we swapped numbers.

At the agent's office was a girl who runs a PR company and I was told she would help me out a lot, and teach me how to get press and how things work. I will always owe them for that.

He then got me Aston Merrygold from JLS. He was a lovely guy and very respectful, you could see he had a good family behind him. I got on really well with him. After I had finished tattooing him he sent a tweet out about him being with me and my phone went mental with girls' texting and calling me asking if I was still with him: it made my twitter go up another 1000 followers.

We planned to meet again in a few weeks' time at a rehearsal studio in South London called Music Bank. It was amazing! Everyone you could think of has played there. When I pulled up there were about 30 girls all gathered round the gates and when I got out the car they all came running over. They knew who I was and were shouting my name and wanting photos with me - all because I had tattooed Aston and was going inside to meet him. I felt a bit of a dick doing it because I was hardly famous, but they all loved me.

When I went in I got talking to one of the guys about working from their studio. I didn't know it at the time but he was the boss. His name was Jimmy Mac, a really cool, tall Scottish guy with a bald head and a big beard.

I ended up doing a lot of work with him over the years, and I started to get press all the time all over the world. People would send me magazines and papers with me in them from all over the place, and Paris Hilton ran stories about me working with some of the acts. It was nuts! I was going out to every country for my work; they would even take stuff from my Instagram without asking me and just make a lot of the stories up from the photos I posted.

I was asked to have a private meeting at a hotel with one of the guys from X Factor. He seemed a nice guy and he started to tell me about his time on the X Factor; he said they didn't want to help him from the start, as they were putting all their time into another act from that year's show. He ended up funding his music himself. I thought this was really sad. He said he had lost his girlfriend over it all and he would go for long walks by the Thames late at night just thinking about when he was on the show.

I started to see a different side to it all. When you go on reality shows like this you don't get a drop of help - they just do what they can to make you big for 5 minutes so they can screw you for every penny they can, and then as soon as the show is over so are the performers' careers, and it really does destroy lives.

Ed asked me if I would pop down again in a couple of weeks and tattoo him and his friend. I told him I would and to get his mate to let me know what he wanted done. About two days later I got a text off a lad who said, "Hi! It's Harry - Ed's friend, just sending you what I want". I told him to just text it over, but it still didn't click at the time who it was. At first he said he wanted a little sketch of a bird; then he said he and Ed wanted Pingu tattooed on them, as they both loved it as kids. I got all the stuff ready, as we were doing it at Harry's house. Then the day before I spoke to Ed and he told me it was Harry Styles that wanted to get inked. He said he had also given my number to Zayn Malik, who called the day before my meeting with Harry.

Zayn said he wanted a stereo on his arm but I didn't have time to get down that day. We looked at doing a different time but he seemed impulsive and he wanted it that day, so it never happened. The next day we went down to Harry's, but at the last minute he changed the address; he said he wanted to do it at his hairdresser's house in North London. I took Tara and Revan with me, since Revan was only about 12 weeks old. When I got there he was waiting outside for me; he seemed a nice lad and the hairdresser was nice too. She had a little girl herself so she and Tara just talked while I got to work. I got started on Ed first, and he had his normal random stuff that meant things to him. Harry was talking to us and was telling me his mate would do random little tattoos on him when he was on tour. He got the machine in a cheap set up from his girlfriend for Christmas. They didn't quite understand the dangers of doing this, so I told him about the regulations and the need for safety, and about how these unlicensed tattooists have no way of cleaning their stuff, and don't know about using fresh needles.

I had a good chat with them about it and he seemed really shocked by what I was telling him. He said he would not be doing it again, and that he just hadn't understood the dangers - like most people don't. I told him of some good places to go if he wanted more stuff doing. I had now finished Ed's tattoos, but Harry had changed his mind about ten times before we even got started. Ed said he wanted to tattoo Harry, so I set it all up ready for him. I know Ed, though – he doesn't listen to advice when it comes to tattooing – and he just went for it. He did him a little lock on his wrist and it looked more like a handbag, but he seemed to love it. I then made a start on Harry's Pingu tattoo. He said he wanted to get 17 Black afterwards on his shoulder, as it was something to do with a gambling reference when he was in Australia.

I got them both done and he took it really well. He said he wanted to look at getting a sleeve and he was looking at birds and flowers, so I said I would send him some ideas. It was really nice to see somebody so big who was so nice and humble; he even signed a card for a one of Tara's friend's 18th birthday, I have big respect for guys like him - still nice and giving people the time of day after being so well known. Some of the acts I have worked with have been so up themselves after one hit single. He asked me not to let anybody know what he'd had done, or show any photos of the tattoo to the press, and I have always stood by my word as regards whatever the client asks me to say or not say.

***

I was not prepared for what was going to happen as a result of all that. I knew One Direction was big but until then I didn't understand how big. I put up a photo with Harry on Instagram before I set off and before I even left London my phone was going mental.

Tara was reading stuff out to me as I was driving. My twitter shot from 7000 followers to over 25000 in less than 3 hours. It was mad, and thinking about it now, I really wasn't ready for it. I didn't have people looking after me like the acts did - I had to figure it all out for myself. I was getting press from all over the world calling me; I had people from China ringing for interviews and girls from all over the world ringing my phone and just screaming and crying trying to ask me what Harry was like.

The next day I sent Harry some art work for a sleeve idea he had, but he said he wasn't going to do that now, he was just going to have bits he wanted as and when he wanted - I think he is a bit impulsive when it comes to getting tattooed! My phone was going off every two minutes; everybody wanted to know what he had done and where, but I couldn't say. This just made them want it all the more. I even got offered 10 grand for the photos by one of the big, well-known newspapers, but I was not going to sell him out. Paris Hilton even ran a story about it all in the States. Girls in America would send me magazines in the post that I had been in, and I would tell them what sort of person he was and what he said but I was not going to say what tattoos he had. Every story they did was twisted a bit. I was getting sick of it all, but for about 3 to 4 weeks that's all the papers were writing about. I just wanted to move on but they wouldn't let it drop. Every story I ever did from that point always ended up about Harry.

I even did a live interview for MTV New York that should have been about my work with Ed but turned back to Harry's stuff: it was starting to take over my career. Then about 3 months later there was a photo that came out of Harry getting tattooed by a friend. It was an old photo from before I met him but they were going to run it like it was a fresh picture and they called me to say they were going to run a story about him being at risk of getting HIV. I was shocked and said, Whoa - wait a moment! You can't run that it just isn't true. He could've got an infection, granted, but HIV was the last thing he could've got. I told them he didn't get tattooed by that guy any more, but they were like a dog with a bone with this story.

I texted Harry about it and told him what they were going to say; he just replied with, "You've got to take the rough with the smooth, Brother!" My name was going to be all over it and I couldn't deal with the bad press from this; Harry could just bounce back but it could have finished me. I told them I would talk to them and get the facts out there. They ran the story the next day, and it was a lot better than what they might have done, but it was still twisted. By now I wanted to get past all the Harry stuff but it just wasn't leaving me, and it ended up a big thing as they still tried to make it sound bad.

Harry texted me that night saying that he wasn't happy about it coming out, and he got a bit arsy over me talking to them, but he didn't understand that I'd only done it to make things sound better for him. At the end of the day I was just a tattooist; I wasn't meant to be dealing with all this press on my own. I never thought that what I had started would get this big so fast. After that all the papers started to run stories saying that I was putting his tattoos down. I never said anything like that at all, and it just kick-started the Harry stuff all over again. I tried to keep my head down for a bit with the press, but then I found out the girl that was doing my press at the agent's office had been pushing the Harry stories all this time. I was pissed off to find out that she was the reason everybody had been getting at me for stories.

I sent her an email saying that I was going to look after my own PR from now on and she didn't even reply, which I found really rude. Don't get me wrong - I owe them so much for all the stuff that I picked up from them and all the people I had met through them, but I could not waste my time just talking about Harry all the time, I needed to move on with my career and not just live being known for tattooing a little thing on Harry Styles.

***

A few days passed and the guy from the music agent's office rang to say that two lads from a show called Made in Chelsea wanted to meet up, I headed down to London again and took my shop apprentice with me. I'd never really watched the show but I knew about it through adverts and from my missus watching it. I had been messaging one of the lads, Oliver Proudlock about what he wanted, so when I got there, I showed him and he was pleased. The other lad that was with him was Jamie Laing. He was bonkers - not from this world he was so posh.

I tattooed Olly first and then Jamie. Jamie said they wanted to get something done the same together. They said it was going to be the words "Lost Boi" and they wanted it on their forearms - they said it was something they called themselves on the show. I did it, and they were both pleased and said they were going to be booking in for more eventually.

***

The guy from Midnight Beast called and asked when was best to come down. I told him that he was welcome to stay at ours and go out for food and drinks with some friends that loved his show and he had spoken to on twitter. He said that would be lovely and when he came down a bunch of us went to this restaurant called Jimmy's: it was an all you could eat - bit tacky like, but nice. We then went on to a pub for a few drinks, but we didn't have a late one, since I was starting his sleeve in the morning. Next day he was really pleased with what I'd done and couldn't wait to come back down for more. He was really nice and polite and I got on with him well.

By now it was coming up to September time and Andy Meakin got back in touch saying JLS were playing a gig at Loughborough University, and to go down, I texted Aston and told him I would be there and he said to come backstage after the show had ended. I took Tara and it was the first time she had met Aston so she was looking forward to it. We watched the gig from a balcony away from the rest of the fans and it was really good to see. As the show ended we made our way back downstairs and went to see the boys in their dressing rooms. Me and Aston talked about meeting up in a few weeks' time and talked about what he wanted to get so I had a rough idea of the things to take down with me.

I was at the music agent's office when they had a call about Frankie Cocozza. All I could hear was, "No, I don't think he would've shit the bed, he must've just stood in something." When he got off the phone he was not happy at all - going up the wall about Frankie. The hotel he was staying in had phoned because they found shit in his room. Frankie was a nice lad, but fuck me he was hard work! About 3 weeks later I met up with him for a tattoo. He was telling me that his mate had some girls around his hotel room one night, and he was getting sick of them going on so he told them to leave. They kept fucking around and wouldn't go; one of them had taken her shoes off, so he told her if they didn't go he was going to shit in her shoe. She still didn't go, so he really did shit in her shoe - in the middle of a hotel room. She soon left after that! He was a sweet lad but sometimes he needed reining in a bit.

Chapter 8

It was about 3 weeks later and Ed asked me if I would come to a few of his gigs in the UK and tattoo him; the first one he had free was Birmingham, so we met at his hotel room. He had been talking about getting a gingerbread man done for a while now after I made a joke about it. He'd already had the word 'red' tattooed on his arm the week before by some guy down south because he had done a song with Taylor Swift for her album *Red*. It was coming out that week so he got the tattoo done to celebrate it. You could see it was still healing. The meeting we had was top secret and there was nobody around outside at all. After I had finished the gingerbread man we did some other little bits to his other tattoos before he had to go get ready for his gig. Before he left I asked him if he would sign a picture that I had drawn to be auctioned off for a charity event, and asked if he would sign a guitar I wanted to put on the wall in the studio. We took photos of him doing it, just to prove it was real and we put them on Instagram.

The next morning it was all over the papers that Ed had got me to tattoo the word 'red' on him to show his love for Taylor Swift! It was insane how they make up this shit without any proof. I ended up getting press all over the States again for something I had not even done. I rang Ed and told him what had been said and he wasn't bothered - luckily he knew it wasn't me. I just panicked at first though, as I really didn't want him to think I had leaked anything to the press. He had been so good to me in helping me with my work and getting me more clients, for me and also just being a good friend.

I'd got back from being with Ed about 3 days and I went to meet Aston at his house. I put his address in my sat-nav and it was down a really long lane in the country-side. It was amazing! There was a huge gym room, and a massive kitchen with a chandelier made up of wine glasses: it was so cool. Tara came with me and was just admiring the decoration. There was no way we could have taken the kids - there were fancy ornaments eve-rywhere. He had a thing for skulls and there were loads of cool decorated ones in most of the rooms.

Aston's a huge fan of Michael Jackson, so we came up with the idea of a tape with the word "bad" coming out of it. It worked out really well and has now turned out to be one of the most copied things I have ever done on a celebrity.

While I was there I asked him if he could sign one of his albums for my friend's daughter. I told him her par-ents had split and she was taking it hard and straight away he said he would give her a quick call. When she picked up and Aston told her it was him I could hear her screaming: it really made her day. I don't usually ask the celebs for things but I know I would do anything for my kids and to make them happy, so I knew what it would mean for my friend to see his daughter happy. Aston's such a lovely guy and he was so pleased to help.

***

One day I got a call from a mate to see if I wanted to go on his act's tour to just hang out. I don't really like going out - I would rather be home with my wife and kids. I love seeing how happy the kids are to see me when I get in and to just relax and see them after being at work all day, but it's good to meet people: you never know who you're going to meet next and what it could lead to, so I went to meet him at a bar in town and he was telling me about how mad the tour had been. They were getting a lot of girls trying to get back stage to the main act and every night he would be fucking something in his dressing room. He showed me lots of photos and said they would have to video stuff because some girls liked to cry rape a lot now, or try and sell stories.

We went back to the gig and the show was about to kick off. It was a really good night and afterwards we went back stage. There were girls everywhere trying to get into his dressing room. The main act came out after a while and he was pretty much pissed by this point. He started having photos with them all and flirting about with some of them. Then he had a photo with this girl who was with her mum. They had been waiting for ages and she must've only been about 18 or 19. He was having a little chat with her for a while, and then he asked her if she wanted to come have a look around back stage. Her mum just sat outside his room next to the door when the daughter went in with him, and they were gone for almost an hour. Her mum was just sat there doing a crossword. It was shocking.

When she finally emerged on her own you could see she was a bit flustered. I got going not long afterwards. The next day my mate called me up; he was telling me that his act was fucking the hell out of her in the room next to where her mum was sat! I could not believe what he was telling me and how bad some girls are these days.

***

I had a week's break and then I was back with Ed. (Well, I say 'break', it was more dealing with non-famous clients). I got a call from Ed Sheeran again asking for me to go on tour with him. I said yes, that would be cool as it was about the only place I had never tattooed him. I started on the Doncaster show. I met him at the hotel, so we just went for Nandos first, and this became the usual thing for us to do. One of Tara's friends should have gone to his Nottingham gig the week before but her grandad had passed away so she could not make it. I told Ed about it, and he said to bring her down and he'd sort out a pass for her.

When we got there we went back stage to his room: it was so chilled out on his tours - like one big happy family. His support acts were in his dressing room and they were really nice and polite and kept talking about tattoos. Tara looked up and there in front of her was Louis Tomlinson from one direction. Ed had invited him to his Doncaster gig, as that's where Louis is from. He seemed a nice lad too; he was with his girl-friend and his mum and stepdad. They all seemed nice, down-to-earth people in that band.

When it was time for Ed to go on Louis told us to stay with him if we wanted. He was asked if he wanted to go hide out the way at the side of the stage so he didn't get mobbed, but he said no - he just wanted to go watch with everybody else. I was stunned! I thought it was really cool that somebody as big as him would do that; most of the other acts I knew definitely wouldn't have. We had two bodyguards to take us down and there were about a thousand people in the crowd. We could see people were clicking it was Louis but they just stuck us the middle of the fans; it was really well planned it ended up being a good night. It was the first gig of Ed's I had seen and I could understand why the fans absolutely love him.

***

MTV had just aired a show called *The Valleys* about a bunch of young adults from the Welsh Valleys and them making better lives for themselves. A contact asked me if I wanted to go down to a party in some nightclub in Mayfair, London as they were doing a PA there. I said yeah, that would be awesome and told them to put mine and Tara's names on the guest list. The day of the party I'd finished work and my shoulder was in agony. I think I'd pulled a muscle and it was a real struggle to drive down to London. I was not looking forward to it at all as I knew we would be in a busy club, and so I took some medication to try and ease up the pain. As soon as we got there I decided to have a vodka and coke, which was my first drink since I met Tara.

It was a really posh club where all the football stars would go - like Ashley Cole. I have never seen anything like it: there were so many girls stood around in there just waiting for rich guys to come in, as you could tell because a lot of them were on their own. They were all dressed to perfection - hair immaculate and all dressed up - like they'd put so much effort into their outfits. They must've done this all the time, just to try and bag rich men or a famous person. It was shocking. I had a chat with Chidgey from the show about his tattoo; there were two of the girls from the show with him and they were so drunk. One of them had a really low cut top on and her tits were almost falling out, and the other one had no knickers on and you could see her minge through the dress. One of them said she wanted to get tattooed but wasn't allowed, as they were strict on the show and they didn't want the cast getting anything done.

It's always shocked me how little these celebrities know what's going on with their lives.

There was some guys sat on the other table near us and I thought I had seen them before, but didn't know where. They had a lot of gold diggers hanging around but they didn't seem too bothered. Later on I was in the toilets and one of these guys came out of a cubicle. He looked a bit sheepish, but then a second one walked out too. There was a guy sat in there giving out aftershave; he just looked at me and laughed and said, "I'm saying nothing!" When I went back out to my table I asked one of the guys who it was on the other table and he turned out to be a footballer - I knew I had seen him before.

A couple of days later I spoke to a mate I had about it all. He told me the footballer was known for being gay, but it could never come out, and that it happened a lot in this game. I think it's really sad that in 2015 you still can't be openly gay. From what I have been told there's loads of people who have to keep their sexuality secret, but most of them just get seen with really hot girls to draw you away from ever thinking they are gay.

***

I got a call from Derry from the Risk to say he wanted to come back up to my studio in Derby. He was coming up on the train so I went to pick him up from the station and he asked if we could go and pick up a girl he knew in town as it was on our way to the studio. I thought she must have been a friend of his or something; she was a skinny blonde girl from Stoke. She had come down on the bus to see him. When she got in the car I could hear them whispering in the back and about 2 minutes later I got a text from him say she wants to suck us both off in the car. I just glanced back at him through the mirror and laughed. When we got to the studio he asked me to give them 5 minutes and he disappeared in the toilet with the girl for about 15 minutes. I couldn't believe it - the land lord was stood outside the toilet door showing new tenants around the building, luckily they moved before they come out. When they come back in the other artist were all working, they all knew what had gone on in the toilet and the girl had no shame at all about any of us knowing.

He showed everybody a video on his phone of what she was had been doing, there must have been about six guys in the studio and he was showing us the video of her sucking him off. She was a proper dirty bitch spitting on his cock then pushing it deep down her throat, it was like watching a cheap porn film and she loved all the guys seeing it, she didn't have any shame at all.

Afterwards she asked if somebody could drop her off at the station as she said she had to go pick up her kid from school and go meet her boyfriend. I couldn't believe what she just said - she had a family and she was doing this with some act of the x-factor!

I got one of my lads to drop her off and whilst in the car she was telling him she had seen I knew Rizzle Kicks. She started telling him that she was at one of their gigs one night and she was trying to get their attention from the crowd, she told him it had been really hot in there and her fake eyelashes were falling onto her cheek so she got nowhere with them. She told him to pass on her details if I saw them again - she basically wanted to just suck them off too. It was shocking how many girls were like this, they would just go to gigs to basically try and do sexual acts with a celebrity!

After we had finished he asked me to come down in a few weeks to one of his gigs as another lad in his group wanted tattooing. They were the supporting act for Peter Andre and the only time I could do was in Oxford. I'd never met Peter Andre so thought it might be a good opportunity - one to see what he's really like, and two it might lead to me possibly tattooing him. When I got there I was told to go round the back to the stage door, where me and Tara stood waiting, as nobody was there yet. While we were waiting Peter's car pulled up by the door, and when he got out he took the time to come round and say hello. At first I thought he must have been told about me being there, but then he started asking me if I was coming to watch the show and talking to me like I was a fan. I told him I wasn't there for that but to tattoo the Risk, the group supporting him. It was quite funny really - I mean, do I look like a Peter Andre fan? But he was nice to me and not a lot of acts would have gone out of their way to come say hello. After chatting he went back round to get his missus out the car and go in.

I never saw them again all night after that, they just kept themselves to themselves. I noticed his manager back-stage giving me dirty looks, which to be honest seemed like they were a bit up themselves. I went for a walk around the front to see the crowd walking in, and I was shocked that most of his fans were really old people and a lot of them were in wheelchairs – so many that they had to take a whole row of chairs out, whereas usually they only need a few wheelchair spaces. I wasn't used to this kind of fan base; I was more used to young girls screaming and jumping about all over the place. When it was time for him to come on I thought I'd watch to see what he was like, but it was pretty corny and I couldn't endure much before I had to leave.

Chapter 9

It was a few weeks before Christmas now, and I was cramming in as much work as I could to make money for bills in case I had a quiet period. Chidgey from the Valleys said he wanted to come up, so I told him to come up one evening and I would work late on him. We got to the studio and made a start on his sleeve, and after we left I told him he could stop at ours. He came down again after a few weeks and some girl drove all the way from Sheffield to meet him: apparently they had been speaking for a few days. He said they were going to the cinema and I gave him a key to get in afterwards. When they came back she ended up sucking him off in her car right outside my house. It makes me laugh how some girls are when it comes to meeting famous people.

After a few days I was back with Ed at his London flat. We were just doing some bits ready for the next date I was back on his tour. He had a friend pop round to let him listen to some new music he'd done. He was a little Indian-looking guy. I didn't have a clue who he was at first and it wasn't really my place to ask, but about 3 weeks later I saw him on TV and then I realised it was

Naughty Boy. Ed said he had a gift for me to say thank you for keeping coming down to him. He gave me his very own gold plaque for selling over a million copies of his album. I could not believe it! - I felt honoured. It was such a nice thing to do. I had such huge respect for this guy. He is the most humble and polite, loving and respectful guy I have ever had the pleasure of meeting. Ed was telling me he was on the X Factor that weekend, so I asked him to tell a guy on it called Arthur to give me a call and I would sort his arms. I had already been asked to do the X Factor tour but I don't like to put all my eggs in the same basket. By now I had made so many contacts and had tattooed so many people in the industry that I was getting to be unstoppable. I was trying to split family life and work, but work was just taking over everything. I was fully aware my wife was doing it all on her own with very little help from me. I would be at home and still be doing nothing to help because I was taking bookings for work or contacting celebrities and TV companies. I had to keep going, but I didn't know what my goals were any more, or what I wanted from it all, apart from the better life for my kids. I got a text about two days later from James Arthur saying that he did want to come see me, so we planned to meet in London one day when the show was over and he was starting the tour in January.

Rizzle Kicks called again and asked me to go back down to his; he told me he had moved house and he wanted me to pop down for some more ink. When I went down to his house it was really cool, and it was handy because it was a few streets away from the music agent's office. He had some mad patterns up his arm so we just added some more stuff to it. I have always had respect for the Rizzle Kicks guys: if it wasn't for them I would not be where I am now.

***

It was now Christmas 2012 and Ed texted me to ask if I would go down. I told him I was taking bookings from the 27th and to let me know when he was going to be free. He said the 27th and 28th would be great, so I made sure I booked those days in. Christmas Eve came and I finally finished my day's work and headed home to my family to enjoy my few days off with them.

On Christmas Morning it was lovely to see the boys' faces when they were opening their presents. Revan couldn't really take much in as he was only 7 months old, but Rocco really enjoyed it, as he had not long turned 2 years old. My dad was down from Leeds for the Christmas and New Year and he came over to Tara's parents for Boxing Day dinner and to see the boys open their presents. I love having family around me at Christmas.

The day after Boxing Day we got in the car to go down to Ed's. The whole family was with me this time - Tara and both boys. He had a few female friends round, so they helped Tara look after the boys while I got to starting a phoenix on Ed's arm.

It was mayhem trying to work with Rocco running around. Ed had this massive alarm near his front door like a panic button type of thing, and I was dreading Rocco touching it. Not only that, but he had a lot of Lego lying around that had taken him ages to build. I just kept thinking, if Rocco touches them they'll break. Ed said he had some Pingu DVDs and put them on for the boys to watch.

He'd said he had got me a little gift for Christmas so I felt compelled to get him something too - but what do you get for a guy that has everything? There was a guy in my studio that made silicon models so he made me a gingerbread man on a stand in the same pose as Ed's tattoo, and I got him a gingerbread man shaped cookie jar. They were more a little novelty gift over anything extravagant. He loved them and laughed when he opened them. Ed ordered us some food - some burgers and pizzas - and after hours of tattooing we finished about 2am. Ed went up to bed and as he had still not furnished his house we slept in one of his bedrooms with a mattress on the floor and bare quilts and pillows.

His house was an amazing size. The kitchen was huge and there were all his homely touches scattered around the place. The next morning we got up and headed back home so I could start back at work that afternoon.

***

After the New Year I was down at the music agent's office again, tattooing the lad that owned it, James Arthur had got in touch and I told him to come down - that was the first time I met him. When he came in you could see he was all insecure about being there: it was like he didn't want to be seen; he was a shy person, and I found this really odd, as he had just won the X Factor. You would think he would be so full of himself, or at least more confident than he was. He really was nothing like the papers tried to make out. I started to tattoo him that night. We didn't do much but we made a start on reworking his sleeve, and we planned to meet back up at Music Bank when the X Factor started rehearsals in about 3 weeks' time. The press was all over me for tattooing James Arthur but instead of positive stories everybody wanted a bad story. It was shocking, he didn't have a chance - all they wanted to print was bad stuff. I did an interview with one of the celeb magazines about it and because there was nothing bad being said about him they didn't run it. I feel sorry for him with the shit he had to go through. You don't get any lessons on how to deal with being a celeb; you're just chucked in at the deep end.

When we met up at Music Bank Union J were the first guys to come up talking to me. They were like kids in a sweet shop! They wanted everything doing - they didn't know what to ask for first. I swapped numbers with all of them apart from Rylan, as he was in the Celebrity Big Brother house. They said they would contact me and arrange for when they had a bit more spare time. James told me where he was touring and said to come along to a few of the shows, and then when they were done tattoo him. We arranged for Manchester and Brighton.

The first one, in Manchester, was pretty cool. As I was getting ready for their rehearsals I knew I had James Arthur and Union J in the bag, I just wanted to see who else I could get. I was hoping for Rylan, as I thought he was going to have a good career. After they finished rehearsing and we got back to the hotel we had them clear out a room so we could tattoo in there and make it safe to work in. James said he wanted to get his hand done and we drew up a king Arthur idea he had. He loved it, but I told him that because hands swell up and he had to play guitar I would only put the outline and background on his hand that night and then finish it up the next time I was with them. I was not back on that tour then for 2 weeks. The first night he went on somebody in his family saw his hand and didn't like him getting it done. I find that having work done on visible places like your hands can be a bit of a head fuck at the best of times, and when his family was saying it and then the papers started having a go, he started to think about lasering it off. This would not have looked good for me one bit! Everybody would have just blamed me, although it was nothing to do with my artwork.

***

When I went to Brighton I sent out a tweet saying I had just got there, and then settled into the hotel with Tara and the boys. It wasn't long before people were tweeting and asking to say hello to Union J and James Arthur. One girl sent me a tweet asking if I would tattoo her while I was there; I said no, sorry but I was just with the X Factor lot this time. She replied with, "I'll have sex with you if you just tattoo me." I didn't know what to say at first. I told Tara and she didn't quite believe it until she'd seen the tweet, and then just laughed, saying "She's keen!" and I replied with, "Fucking hell, they're friendly in Brighton!" She kept tweeting for about an hour offering sex. It really does shock me what some women will do just to be close to a pop star or have some form of link with them. Someone told me on the tour that Christopher Maloney from that year's show slept with Katie Price's ex-husband Alex Reid that night in the hotel. I don't know if there was any truth to the story but I could tell there was an atmosphere when Christopher was around.

The plan was to tattoo James and finish his hand, but he was so busy rehearsing I just made a start on JJ from Union J. He was such a nice lad - knew just what he wanted and how he wanted it. He had an angel at the top of his arm. We did it after their gig, which meant we didn't get started until about 11.30 at night and finished at gone 3 in the morning: I was absolutely fucked; I needed sleep. Just before I was finished two lads came up to me from Syco, which is Simon Cowell's label, to ask if I would do them some little tattoos. I said I couldn't do it tonight, but I would get up about 6/7 that morning to do it for them before they left. They agreed and said they would meet in that same room at that time before they left.

I met them as arranged and did them before I had to drive 3 hours back home. By now my hectic schedule was really starting to catch up with me; I'd had no proper sleep in a few days and I was stressing about paying bills all the time, since being self-employed you can't take for granted people when people want to walk through the door.

A few days after this I took Tara to watch the show in Nottingham, where we finally got to meet Rylan. He said he wanted some tattoos doing but would book in when he wasn't so busy. I never heard from him again.

Chapter 10

It was getting into March now and I was back down the music agent's office again. I'd had a phone call the day before from a lad called Scott from the boyband 5. He said he was doing the big reunion show and wanted to sort his tattoos out, so I told him I was back down London the next day and to meet up after I'd done my few meetings in the morning.

We got to the office and I was tattooing Jamie Laing again from Made in Chelsea. He said he wanted a silhouette of Peter Pan on his inner arm. I tried to advise him against it, as I thought it was just a shit idea that he would regret, but he said that's what he really wanted, so I just had to do what he asked for. Of course, I can only do what you ask for and do it properly; it's not my job to say you shouldn't have it. As soon as we finished it he had to go film for the next season of the show, and I didn't know for a couple of months until it was aired on TV that he slagged it off while filming and only minutes after having it done, I was not happy about it as he tweeted that it was me that did it, but I thought I'd let it go - it was a one off. But then he started to bitch about it in the celebrity magazines, so I sent him a public message on twitter, saying "If you're going to bitch about the tattoo make sure you tell people I told you not to get it done, because if I see any more press about it then I will tell them myself." He sent me a private message straight away saying, "It's all good Bro. They made me say it on the show for laughs." I told him it wasn't that funny for me as I'd get the bad name for doing it, and he said he was sorry and left it at that. I don't think he actually meant anything bad by it. He just doesn't live in the same world as us. I think all his problems are sorted for him.

The meeting with Scott went well. We met up for lunch in this little pizza place in Leicester Square and he told me what he wanted doing and showed me all the existing work he wanted to get reworked. I told him to contact me when he wasn't as busy as he was then, and I would sort a date for coming down to tattoo him.

After I got back home I decided I wanted to do something positive with my new found notoriety and constant media attention. I had slowly become a beacon for girls that were always asking me to tattoo them - girls as young as 13 asking if they could have the same tattoo as Harry or the same tattoo as Ed. I was telling them that when they were 18 and they were finally of age to get tattooed they would more than likely have changed their minds about what they wanted, and not to rush into getting stuff done. I had parents contacting me saying their daughter or son was a huge fan and with their consent could I you tattoo them. After constantly trying to tell these people the legal age was 18, and about the dangers of going to people that would tattoo them from their houses, I decided to try and get some stricter laws within the tattoo industry. It was going down the pan anyway, there were so many back-street artists working from home that had no idea of clinical waste, hygiene and the importance of sterilising everywhere.

The problem had stemmed from tattoo shows like London Ink, which was making every Tom, Dick and Harry want to learn how to tattoo. How easy it was to buy equipment - and not even good equipment - off eBay was killing the trade. Every genuine professional artist wanted something done but nobody would listen to them.

All I wanted was to make sure that everybody was tattooing by the same rules as the people that worked from reputable studios; that way everybody would have to get registered and licensed to tattoo, aware of clinical waste knowing about insurance, and with a high standard of hygiene for cleaning. This would shut most of the home tattooists down and make things a lot safer. I emailed loads of the top artists in the UK telling them what I was going to do. Half of them didn't even reply and the other half said I wouldn't get anywhere, and that what I was doing wasn't achievable. I have always hated it when people tell me I can't do something - it just spurs me on harder and harder to prove these people wrong.

Meanwhile, the industry was having a huge problem with people tattooing from home, a lot of them in seriously unsafe conditions: people whose dogs were loose around them while tattooing; people making food in the same room as where the tattoo was being done. It was shocking how anyone would go to these places to save themselves no more than £20, but putting themselves at risk of serious diseases for the sake of it. I set up a Facebook page called Tattoo Regulations 2013, and I also contacted our local MP and told the Derby Telegraph what I was doing. It was a huge hit straight away, I told all the celebs that I had worked with to tweet about what I was doing and they were all 100 percent behind it, since it was their fans that were getting the bad tattoos done.

***

After about 2 days it went mental! I had radio shows asking me to come in and do talks, and all the national papers ran a story on it, saying 'Ed Sheeran Backing Tattoo Regulations 2013' and such.

Naturally the haters slowly started to creep in from the people that I was trying to ban and get stopped from working at home. I gathered hundreds of supporters, but for every hundred there were at least 30 people telling me what I was doing was wrong. I received death threats - people threatening to smash my head in, hunt me down at my home and murder me. One guy even set up a hate page calling it 'We Hate Kevin Paul'. That was pretty funny to be honest! They would try and have real personal digs at me, but I couldn't care less what they said, it made me more determined to succeed in what I was doing.

I got a call from a girl off the X Factor called Lucy Spraggan, who asked me to go down to London to meet her at her Management Quest office. It was so nice in there: it was the building that Stella McCartney starting making clothing in. They also looked after Liam

Gallagher and they were telling me tales of what he was really like. I had really upped my game with my contact list now, and I ended up doing a lot of work on Lucy. I got on with her really well; she was quite a nice girl.

Another call came from a guy off a TV show called *The Only Way is Essex*. I'd met him before when Lal Hardy down at New Wave had been tattooed. I went down to his house in Essex and it was a really nice place; he lived in a converted stable at the back of his dad's house. I did a design popular with most music acts, the old-school microphone with roses. It looked really cool, but as soon as he put it on his twitter he was getting loads of hate - people calling it shit and saying it looked like a toaster. We just found it funny though: you can't take anything to heart when dicks online say shit; it's jealousy at the end of the day. I knew it looked good, he knew it looked good and lots of his actual fans out there loved it.

I got on with him really well. He seemed a nice guy, not too cocky and admitting he'd had an easy life. He had been off the show for a bit now and people were starting to forget about him, you could tell that by the lack of press interest in him getting tattooed. But I liked him, and he came up the studio a couple of times too.

***

The regulations campaign was still gathering a lot of attention, and I had a call asking if I would go down to be on Daybreak on ITV. They asked me to find someone who worked from home to tell their side of story. When the day came I went down and met Lorraine Kelly, who was really lovely and flirty natured. It was funny - I just kept thinking of Bo' Selector and now I could see how they made the comparison. I kept getting a visual image of her flicking her legs across and showing her minge.

Anyway, they showed an undercover video of the unregistered home of a guy tattooing and it really got the point across, but then when it switched to the sofa with Lorraine Kelly and Aled Jones, we had to look at some photos. They showed 3 photos live on air and I could not believe it: they had put two really bad photos up showing awful work, but the third one was by my friend Jason Butcher's girlfriend. I wasn't happy - it was such a fuck up – but it was too late for me to say anything about it by time it had gone out. As soon as I got off air I told them what they had done and they took it off their website so it couldn't be seen again.

***

Scott from Five had contacted me and asked me to go down and tattoo him. I went round and also did a little tattoo for his wife. They're such a lovely family, really down to earth and polite, and I ended up really good friends with him. He told me loads of stories about when Five was at the top; he told me about when they worked with Queen and about when he met Liam Gallagher and got pissed with him in Rio. Liam was telling him how he had just split up with his wife, Patsy Kensit. He kept telling Scott she was a cunt, then turning to Scott's wife and saying, "No offence, Love!" Scott said he was the most down-to-earth guy you would ever meet. They were playing Bop It in his hotel room, pissed out of their heads, and every time Liam did it wrong he just said, "Fuck It!" and started again. It was so funny to hear – growing up in my teens I always loved Oasis.

The following week Channel 5 News contacted me and asked me to go on and do an interview about the regulations. I didn't realise it was going out live so wasn't really thinking about watching what I said and not swearing: that's the hardest part of doing radio and TV live.

Next day I had a phone interview with Radio One, to go out on air the following week. I was warning people about letting friends tattoo you at parties, or just because they'd bought a kit off eBay.

Environmental health in London called that day too, wanting a meeting to talk about what I was trying to do. When I did the meeting at the end of the week, we started to talk about what I wanted to see happen, but they didn't seem to really care about the tattoo industry. The woman I was speaking to informed me the law was only 16 to get tattooed. My jaw dropped, and I just sighed. These people were in charge of environmental health and she didn't even have a clue what the actual age for getting a tattoo was. I could see I had my work cut out: it took me over 20 minutes before she would understand that it was 18, and that was only after she got someone to look up the law on the internet!

We ended the meeting positively and arranged a second meeting to get the ball rolling and start making changes. I was really happy with what I had done and that I'd managed to do it on my own too. I had never really succeeded in anything before and after my past I didn't ever imagine me mixing with people like this.

A couple of days later I got a call from Ray Quinn. He said he wanted to come down and get his first tattoo; he wanted to start a sleeve. It was the basic idea that most people come with - angels and clouds - but we came up with our own way of doing it all. I told him I was sick of everybody coming in having the same old thing done over and over again, and he appreciated that and was happy for me to make a twist on it. He was a nice guy, a really happy chap. I was looking forward to doing this, as when I was growing up I used to watch Brookside with my granddad back in Leeds. I'm sure he would've loved that if he was still alive. When we started to put the design on him, he had to text his missus a photo of what we were going to do. I did think it was a bit odd at first, but then everybody is different. We would have to wait for her reply before he would start the tattoo, and sometimes it would be about 20 minutes before she did. It was nuts! I could see she had his balls firmly in her hand; it was like he was scared of her or something. When I met her she seemed a nice girl - I mean, she wasn't happy about him wanting to get a lot of tattoos, but she was nice none the less. He would come up and sneak a bit more ink onto his arm, and this went on for ages until he'd got most of his arm done. He ended up getting a lot of press over this new rougher image he now had.

I was finding out now that more and more people were thinking that you had to be famous to get tattooed by me, or people would say, how did you ever get booked in with him? - thinking that I was booked up for years and charged ridiculous prices that only the rich could pay for. This was far from the truth.

Chapter 11

I was asked by Luke Williams, the guy from Warner Brothers, to do a charity football match called Soccer Six; he sent me a text asking if I was playing. I knew what it was, as I had seen it on TV on the Dappy's N-Dubz Show. I had never played football before in my life but I was really up for it. I had not been asked or told anything about it, but he said he would get me in it. It wasn't for about 4 weeks, so I just carried on with the rest of the work I had to do.

I was filming a documentary for BBC One about the tattoo regulations thing, and it was mental! I was trying to keep my studio open all by myself whilst filming for TV shows and coping with the rest of the media plans I was involved in. I was still getting hate from some people over changing the laws, but I was all about keeping good energy around me: I hate having bad feelings it makes for bad Karma. I was slowly starting to get spotted in public places; people would do double takes or whisper as I walked past saying, "that's him!" That was the only problem with being 6ft 4 and having face tattoos. I got a call asking if I was going to play in the celebrity football match, Soccer Six. I told Luke, who'd already asked me about it, that I wouldn't just come to play football, but I would help towards something for the raffle that night. I said I would draw portraits of some of the celebrities that were playing in the charity match, and I did Dappy and a few others. On the day, I took my oldest son Dennon and some friends came with Tara and our Rocco: he was getting on for just over 2 and half years old, so he was getting to that age where he would enjoy things more.

Off I went to go and get changed into my football gear and I was hoping I would get to meet Dappy and tell him I would tattoo him; he came into the dressing room and kept looking over, but didn't say anything. We went out and played our matches; it was a number of rounds we had to win and I got to the final with my team, I haven't a clue how!

After we finished and all the celebs were changed again, it was the after-show entertainment. I had to go find Dappy to get him to sign his picture and it was mental - I have never seen fans go as crazy for anyone like they do for Dappy.

I left Tara and Rocco with our friends and me and Dennon went to get Dappy. I finally got hold of him and his management and we headed towards the lift to go up to the VIP area, but every time we tried to talk he kept getting distracted by one of the fans trying to get to him. He told me he was sorry, and to bear with him a moment. He was telling his management and security that he couldn't just leave this poor girl stood there crying; his security were trying to say no and to just go upstairs, but Dappy stood his ground and he got her in the lift. She was so happy to have met him and was trying to control herself for a photo with him. I thought to myself what a lovely guy - putting his fans first.

We had a chat and he invited me to go down and stay with him for a week, but I told him I wouldn't be able to be away from work that long. But we swapped numbers and I got his security's number as well, as he said if I couldn't contact him I could go through him as he would always be with him. He asked if I was playing the second Soccer Six a week later; I said yeah and would see him there again.

***

The next week it was in Reading and we did the same kind of thing, but this time I had the camera crew with me for the BBC One documentary I was filming. I took them onto the pitch with me and was speaking with all the players about the tattoo regulations.

I met up with Dappy in the VIP area again and Tara got to talking with his missus. They got on really well as they both have two boys, so they had plenty in common, and we arranged to go round the following weekend.

It was my birthday and I had all the family with me. I got to Dappy's house and Boy, was it lovely! - a real nice barn conversion and so homely for the kids. My boys and his were playing and Dappy and his missus kept laughing at Revan. He had just turned one and they nicknamed him 'Marshy'; they said he looked like a little fat marshmallow man. He even got me a birthday cake. He was a really lovely man. Dappy told me what he wanted and I sat round his for hours drawing his artwork to perfection, confirming with him what he wanted and making changes. Every time I finished he would change his mind and say he wanted something else tweaking on it. When it was finally drawn up and completed he was so happy with it and arranged to come and have it done during that week.

It was 3 days later when he and his family came down, and Tara took his missus and kids out for the day while I tattooed him. We started the pin up down his leg but he didn't sit very well for it. We kept stop-starting all the way through and we left it with half of it to do the next time he would come up. We headed back to mine to pick up his missus up and he insisted he came in and had food with us all, seeing as we hadn't eaten anything all day while we were working. He went straight to his missus and kids to give them hugs and then made sure he told Tara how grateful to her he was for looking after his family for the day.

Any time he visited he left he always made sure he said a nice goodbye, and was polite as anyone could be. He's really not as bad as the papers make him out to be.

***

About this time one of the acts I had already tattooed from a reality show called me up. I assumed he wanted to book in for more on his tattoo but he wanted a chat about his situation. He was telling me that he'd had a falling out with his dad, and he had met a girl from another country. His management had stopped looking after him and he only had about a £1,000 to his name. I was stunned. How could someone from a show like that be so poor! He didn't have any contacts in the entertainment world, so I gave him some advice. I was just a tattooist, but I already had so many links in this entertainment game.

***

After doing Soccer Six a few weeks before, a lad called Nathan who worked there contacted me, saying he wanted to leave and was looking to start managing people. He said he had some good links and knew some useful people, so I took his word for it. I thought if he worked at Soccer Six he must know what he was doing, and I let him start running all my meetings in London. He was living down there, so it would save me going down all the time. It also gave me a bit more time with my family.

I was starting to think that with my contacts and Nathan's previous work with Soccer Six we could help the guy from the reality show to get back on his feet. He said he would like to do his own sitcom based around a gym in Essex and I said I knew a company I had been working with that would be up for something like that. Nathan and I arranged a meeting for us all. It went really well and they were up for doing it; all I needed to do now was sort his short-term money problems.

One day we went to the Gilgamesh Restaurant, Camden and we were chatting about it all and how it was going. I slowly began to see that Nathan was trying to hold things back from me. I would help him out loads: he would stop at my house, he came to my studio, and I tattooed him as well, but he was cutting me out of deals that I had set up in the first place. That's the only problem with this industry - everybody is out to fuck you over.

I don't think it was the client's doing - he was a nice guy - it was the cunt from Soccer Six that I tried to help.

I had always got on with the guy that owned Soccer Six. I think they had a lucky escape getting rid of Nathan when they did. Before long I found out that the lad from the reality show was fucked over by Nathan too. I dropped him a link about it so he had a heads up what a cock he was dealing with. I do believe things like this are better left off to Karma. From what I hear the lad from the reality show has now got legitimate management behind him and that dickhead Nathan is in some dead end job in Lidl!

***

I was on my way home from a day in Parliament about the tattoo regulations and changing the laws when a music link I had met before asked if I could come up to him that night in Manchester and tattoo him. He said he was leaving that weekend to go on tour in Europe and this was the only time he had free, I told him it wasn't a problem but I was coming from London, so not to expect me there for a bit. He said ok and then told me who he was on tour with - Rhianna! I was excited at the thought of being around someone so big who also gets a fair amount of ink: I thought hopefully it would be an amazing chance. When I got there I had to go meet her band first in a bar in town; by that point they were all half pissed, but they all seemed nice - really loud, but most Americans are I find.

When we got to the venue I had never seen anything like it. Each dressing room had a 60inch TV and games system. There was a gym and a drum kit as well. Most acts just have a bowl of fruit, or some chocolates and alcohol. I ended up tattooing two of the guys in the band and by time we had finished it was time for them to go watch the gig. Rhianna's assistant came and asked me if I wanted to watch because Rhianna knew I was there and did want to meet, so I went to watch the show from around the front. I was so shocked at how dirty she was on stage and how many young girls were trying to copy her, but it was a good show - one of the best I have seen.

When I went back-stage afterwards I saw her guitarist walk past and I could not believe who it was. I had to do a double take but my eyes weren't deceiving me: it was Nano Bettencourt from the 90s band, Extreme. I absolutely fucking loved them back in the day. That was way better any time than meeting Rhianna! I had a photo with him, then I ended up leaving there about 2 in the morning and driving all the way back to Derby - I was fucked!

***

After doing the tattoo regulation thing I got asked to do a talk in a school in Newhall where I'd spent a lot of my time as a kid. I thought it was funny how I never went to school when I was a kid and now I'd been asked to go back and talk about stuff. When I got there I didn't know what to think about it, or what I was going to say but I could see it was going to be hard work. It was a rough place to be brought up, and most of the kids there had an attitude problem from the start. I had been doing some work over the regs with Capital FM Radio for a about a month, so when I told them they jumped at the chance to come to the school with me.

I got them to fill out a questionnaire about tattooing: we put everything from how old do you have to be to get tattooed, to do you know anybody with a tattoo who is still at school; it was shocking how many kids at that school were already tattooed. After we did the talk we got them all drawing tattoo art work and they'd started to warm to me by then. Of course, they all just wanted to ask me about celebrities and one of them just asked me if I was rich.

When we had finished the Capital FM reporter asked some of the kids what they thought to my talk, and I was amazed that they'd actually taken in what I had said. One 14 year old lad was telling us that his mum was trying to get him to let his uncle tattoo him with a shit machine he had off eBay. It was really shocking how bad it had got in the industry.

***

I was slowly starting to get a ton of different kinds of famous people contacting me. It was getting ridiculous: near on every day someone would either message me on twitter or call me.

One call was from a well-known RnB act about getting a tattoo and he was all cocky on the phone from as soon as I picked up the phone to him. He was telling me what he wanted, and that it had to be done on this set day, and that he was going to be drinking and smoking

When we was leaving the Hotel and we realised we were on Route 66.

When I Tattooed Adam Ant on Paddy Condiside.
(Photo by Jules)

Ed Sheeran Tattooing Harry Styles.

Me and Paddy Considine.

Ed Sheeran with Ginger Balls.

Me and Frankie Cocozza.

A Picture of Paddy's Arm.

Me with Harry Styles.

Me with David Hasselhoff.

Me with Vern Troyer.

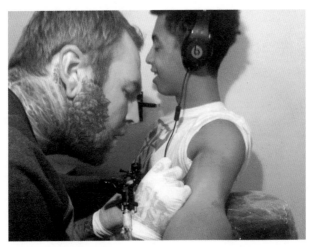

Tattooing Jordan's Fox.

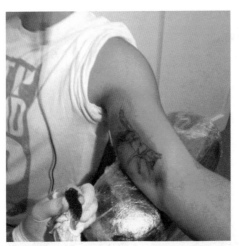

Jordan from Rizzle Kicks arm. I did a little fox on him as it was something quite personal to him.

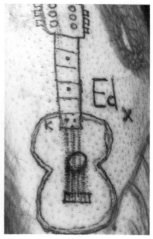

My son Dennon with Dynamo.

The Tattoo Ed Sheeran did of his guitar on my leg.

Radio One Interview for Tattoo Regulations 2013.

The gold Plaque Ed Sheeran gave me to thanks for doing his tattoos.

When I Tattooed James Arthur his Kind Arthur on his hand.

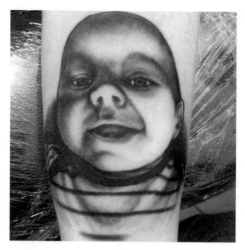

This is the tattoo I did of the baby that died. This makes me cry when I look at this pic now.

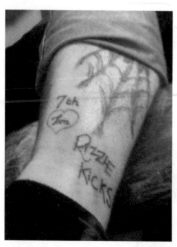

The Tattoo Rizzle Kicks did on my leg next to the two tattoos Tara did.

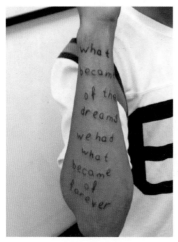

What Harley from the Band Rizzle Kicks had done when he came up to the studio.

When Derry from the Risk visited.

When I did Soccer Six in 2013 with the X-Factor Guys. Big Thanks to Mark for letting me take part in this.

Tara with Revan last year at London Tattoo convention aged 2.

Tattooing Ray Quinn in his Ex-Managers pub.

In Duke of Hamilton with Ruth Killeen, Lucy Hilbert, Kevin Paul, Ray Quinn, Aurora Dawn & Lilly Say (Author).

In Parliament with Ray Quinn, Lucy Hilbert & Clifford Marker.

weed. He also told me not to tell anybody, as my studio would not be able to handle his following: he was a right dick. I told him if he was going to get tattooed by me he would definitely not going to be drinking or smoking in my studio! He got a bit arsy - kept telling me about who he was. I knew he was a big act, but after doing people like Harry and Ed I didn't need to put up with people's shit anymore. I was a professional tattoo artist with a good reputation after doing all the tattoo regulation stuff. I didn't need this shit and I was starting to lose interest in doing it all now anyway; it really drained me and I was rarely seeing my family.

I soon got asked to tattoo the other guys from Union J, meeting them at a penthouse in Camden - it was so nice, overlooking the whole of the lock and market - and I ended up tattooing all of them. The two lads that I hadn't already tattooed only had small tattoos. They were tweeting about it as it was all going on, saying they were with me, tagging me in photos. The next thing I know my phone was ringing: it was my landlord from the building my studio was in saying they had families camped outside because they thought it was being done there! They even tried to kick the front door lock off to check, so somebody had to let them in just to prove that my studio was locked up. My life was just getting madder every day; I was being asked to do so many things, I couldn't take it all in.

One music act I was working with asked me to go round to his house privately, as he didn't want anybody to know about what we were doing, so nobody knows to this day that I tattooed them. Their house was amazing; he told me he paid 1.2million for this pad in the countryside. It was really cool - fully kitted out with big screen TV's and a cinema room. I would love a house like that for my boys to grow up in. When I got there his missus was just leaving with her sister. He had just got back from his UK tour and was telling his manager and me about the gig he did the night before. He said he and his mates got a girl backstage from the gig. This didn't shock me any more, as I knew it was something quite normal to happen on tours. But this time when he got talking to her she told him she was a police officer. She was up for some fun though, and he ended up getting pissed with her and his friends. One thing led to another and he showed us a video on his phone of him and 3 of his friend fucking her. She was saying, don't do that I'm an officer. She was a petite blonde girl and looked like she was in her mid 20s. I could not believe the video! They were pouring beer into her pussy, and then making her stand up so they could drink it as it trickled out of her. He said he always taped anything like that because so many girls would scream rape after they'd spent a night with them.

***

There was a girl I knew through Luke Williams who was the niece of Kim Wilde. I'd tattooed her and her dad before, so knew them quite well - they were a lovely family. They had invited me to a charity ball they were hosting, and asked if I could help them out in any way possible. I told them I would donate a signed piece of artwork and a day's work with me to go up on the raffle. I also wondered if I could get any celebrities to come and help, so got in touch with a few I thought would be good. The first one I contacted was Ray Quinn. I asked him to contact Rikki, Kim's brother about it and to say I'd told him about it, which he did. The next day he said he was going to be singing with Marty Wilde!

We were told it was suits and ball gowns and to dress very smart. On the night they were raffling all sorts of prize off: holidays, apprenticeships, and fancy dinners - all sorts of amazing things. It was going towards a local breast cancer clinic that helped Rikki's wife and mother overcome the disease. On the night, I was having to mingle with all these celebs and I noticed Rick Astley: I was in awe - I love his music – and I finally got a photo with him near the end of the night. Ray was up singing with Marty Wilde, so we were sat with his missus. She was a nice girl and again she and Tara just sat talking about the kids all night. It was a really nice night: there was a number of celebs there; 80s bands, presenters, and mainly close friends of the Wilde family within the industry. We left the party way before it ended because we were getting tired now. I got to speak with some more of Rikki's family and they said they were coming up for more tattoos and they really loved my work.

Ray was thankful I'd got him the gig. He really enjoyed himself too, and everyone loved his duet with Marty Wilde. I even got to meet Rick Astley, which was so cool. I fucking loved him as a kid and I never thought I would ever meet people like that.

***

I got a call from some local lads wanting to come get some work done. One of them wanted to get a lion on his leg and the other wanted to start a sleeve; I didn't know it at the time but they played for Derby County Football Club. I tattooed Johnny Russell first - he had the lion on his leg. He seemed a nice lad, but he was really quiet to start off with and I didn't really follow football so didn't know what to say at first. After he had been in a couple of times he started to open up a bit. He turned out to be a big trainers lover like me, so we would normally talk about that. I had the other guy, Jeff Hendricks, come in a week or so later for his first tattoo. He wanted to start big and get a sleeve, so we began with his lower arm and he got a big pin up with tattoos. It looked really cool - most footballers just got clouds and angels.

I hadn't understood how big a deal it was to the locals about Derby players, but it ended up going in the local paper about them coming in. People were emailing and texting me saying how cool it was, how proud they were that I was tattooing the Derby boys, and how I'd finally made it. It was crazy! I had been tattooing a list of celebrities for years and none of them said anything, then I do some local players and everybody goes nuts. It was really mad how two years ago I could not even make contact with a celebrity, but now my phone was full of them: it was so easy to get anybody I wanted. I went round and met all Jeff's family a couple of times; he was just like the guy next door, nothing famous about him at all.

As I say, it was funny how hard it was to get a celebrity client at first, but now I could get one at the click of a finger. I had Paddy Considine want to come back in for some more work; he wanted to get a portrait of Adam Ant this time and he picked a real cool design of him back in the 80s. When we started it he was telling me how he was a big fan of his; I told him my mate in London had a link to him and I was sure I remembered him telling me he knew his manager. I told Paddy I could get a meet with him and he said he would love that, but I don't think he thought I could pull it off. I had a lot of fun with his tattoo – he's got by far the best celeb work I have ever done. I also managed the link to Adam Ant and they ended up friends.

Chapter 12

One day I had a call from Phil, a producer that I'd met a while ago. He wanted me to go down to London for a drink and a catch up. When I got there he was with a guy called Mark Hassell, who is basically the main guy in adult magazines for the UK porn industry. I got talking to Mark about the stuff he does and he told me he was sorting the Paul Raymond Porn Magazine Awards. He asked me if I would give out one of the awards at the show and he also wanted me to help get some other acts to do the same, so I linked him up with some of the lads I had worked with. A lot of them said their management wouldn't agree but a few were really up for it.

On the night of the show I went down with Tara. We'd been told to dress smartly, and that they treat it like the Oscars of the porn industry, so Tara was expecting everyone all dolled up in relatively designer gear. I didn't know what to expect, but when we went in it was not as bad as you would think. The girls who were up for awards were wearing clothes cheaper than Primark; granted we did see a lot of tit hanging out, but you didn't see a single blowjob being handed out all night.

I hate having to get on stage and do stuff like that, so I was dreading going up to give an award out. I just wanted it over and done with. The guy that was hosting the awards and introducing everyone was a Keith Lemon look-alike. He was awful! He had everyone laughing, but they were only laughing because he was shocking. When I went up to name the winner for the award I was giving out - I think it was Milf of the Year - I had to have photos with her and hand her the award; luckily that was all that I needed to do. I went back and sat down with Tara and we stayed for about an hour after the Awards finished, and then went back to the hotel with pizza and just relaxed on the bed. We are both much happier sat in watching films and cosying up together than out on the lash at parties and such.

***

Not long after this, Dappy called saying he had just split up with the mother of his kids and he wanted to come back up. He arrived with two bodyguards, having put it all over twitter that he was coming up to Derby to get tattooed! It was going mental, with girls tweeting saying they wanted to see him. When he got to the studio he was bouncing off the walls, like a hyper child let loose in a sweet shop.

After about an hour we finally got him in the chair, and he took the tattoo ok at first but he just couldn't sit still for long. He told me that some girls were going to pop down from Nottingham to see him and I assumed that he must've known them, but it turned out they were just fans. When they got here he was just chatting with them while we were tattooing him. Then about

20 minutes later he nipped out for a fag with one of the girls and he was gone a good 20 minutes before he came back in. He popped his head round the door and asked if I had another room he could use for a minute, so I let him into the gym room that I have at my studio. Around 20 minutes passed and I wondered where the hell they were, so I went to go see what he was up too. As I left the room I could hear the girl screaming - she sounded like she was being murdered. My studio then was in a building made up of lots of rooms that were rented out as studios. The room next to my gym was rented out to a guy who made knives, (the business was called Block Knives.) When I went to see what Dappy was doing I could see the Block Knives guy sat at his front door just listening to the screams coming from the gym. I said, "I'm so sorry about this," but he just said, "No – it's cool! Never seen anything like this in my life!"

The next thing, Dappy comes running out the room naked, screaming and laughing. His dick was flopping all over the place; it looked abnormal on somebody so small and it reminded me of the video of the woman that got fucked by a horse. I love him to bits, but he is hard work at times. Anyway, Dappy starting running around the building naked while his guards were trying to catch him, to get him dressed before anybody saw. After the girls had left and we finished the tattoo, Dappy wanted as usual to come back to mine to see Tara and the boys. He was good like that, and always put family first.

***

It was the end of November now and I got approached by one of my clients asking if I could tattoo him the first week in December. I said yeah, and that I would book him in, but then he said it would be in his New York house. This might sound really cool, but to me it was just a massive pain in the arse. I really didn't see the point of flying all that way when there were so many good artists already out there. I said I would do it though if they paid for me and my wife to fly out and they paid for our hotel. I thought this would put them off, but it didn't - they just said yes, not a problem. We'll book it tomorrow. I loved New York anyway; it was mine and Tara's favourite place. We arranged for Tara's parents to look after the kids for the weekend while we went over there to do the work, and we made a weekend of it.

I really could not be arsed with working after the flight we had just been on, but it was paying for all this so I just got on with it. It didn't take long - he just wanted music notes and an old-school microphone like they all have. He was a rap artist from the States and he seemed a nice guy, but I can't be doing with all that rap lingo they all use and smoking weed: it's really not me at all. There was a massive bag of cocaine in his room for everybody to use. It really was a different world to the tours I have been on in the UK. The American tours always seem more secure, with body guards on every door, and you can't get anywhere without showing your ID.

As soon as I got done we got going. I was really tired by that point and I could not wait for the next day around New York. Tara had booked a day's sight-seeing tour and normally I didn't really like doing stuff like that, but this time I really did have fun. It turned into the best trip I ever had. We went up to the top of the Empire State Building and Tara got talking to everyone. I love that about her – she'll just turn around and start talking to everyone, telling stories and stuff. I imagine they think, what *is* she on about! But it's nice how fresh and loving she is to the world. After that we went to a sea, air and space museum. We got to see Concord and the first space shuttle, which was really cool. The tour then took us on a boat past the Statue of Liberty and down to the 9/11 site. It was so peaceful there, and everyone just had a sombre look on their face until they exited the grounds. Instead of carrying on with the tour, Tara had told this Scottish couple that we were going to hunt down the Ghostbuster building and they said they would come with us. It was weird to see! I loved watching Ghostbusters when I was younger, and now it was weird to be stood outside it. We then did a little bit of shopping before it was time to fly back home. I really enjoyed it out there.

***

We had only been back a few days and Tara begged for us to put the Christmas tree up. It was the first week in December and I thought it was far too early but she insisted for the kids.

Andy Meakin contacted me again, my friend from Loughborough Uni, and asked if I wanted to go meet Verne Troyer at a gig they were doing. (He played Mini Me in Austin Powers). I jumped at the chance to go say hi and went down a few nights later. It was a bit odd that lots of the students knew who I was now! I had to go meet Verne at about midnight in his dressing room and when I was waiting to go in I could see him sat on his little mobility scooter. He had a big jug of beer he was sucking through a straw - he looked like a little koala bear sat there. When I went in he was so nice to me, telling me about his tattoos. He asked for my twitter name and said he wanted to hook up when he came back to the UK. He started to show me all his ink, telling me stories of why he had them done, which was all to do with films he had been in. I was so shocked by just how small he really was: my 2 year old son was bigger than him.

A couple of days later he went over to Ireland for a gig. I had people contacting me saying that Verne had been talking about meeting me to people over there: it was so nice of him to tell people about me. He was a big Hollywood star at the end of the day and I was an uneducated kid from the Midlands; people like me were not meant to be mixing with people like that. The more stuff like this happened to me, the more I believed in Karma as I would bend over backwards to help people. I really was so grateful for the life I had now, after so many years of hell with my ex. I loved my family so much: I just wanted to give them the best life I could.

I got a call from Dappy saying he was going in the Celebrity Big Brother house. He wanted to try finish off his sleeve and he kept asking me to tattoo his face too. I was never really into doing his face as I knew people would copy it. His driver left us on our own and we had a good heart to heart that night: he told me about his up-bringing and how hard he'd had it, and I could see he still missed his dad. He was telling me how he would spend all his time and money trying to help his friends out and how most people ended up fucking him over or trying to sell stories about him. I thought this was really sad, as he was such a nice lad deep down. He had a big heart and he just wanted people to like him. He was really worried about going into Big Brother because he'd had so much bad press and he didn't want the public to turn on him again.

When his driver came back it was about half 2 in the morning, but Dappy begged me to do a little tattoo under his eye; he wanted a hash tag symbol, as that was going to be his new thing to rap about. After he left I was really worried about how he was going to get on in the Big Brother house. I had a lot of time for him and I saw him as a close friend.

***

It was now Christmas Week and I was doing my usual cramming in as much work as I could. The TV phone calls were still coming in, and Ed called and asked me to go to his just after Christmas Day again. Also, a few TV shows got in touch about the work I had been filming in the summer: it was finally going to be aired in January February time.

A lot of families work Christmas Eve at the latest and then have a good week or two off for Christmas, but I work right up until late evening Christmas Eve and then I am usually back at work the day after Boxing Day.

Christmas morning came and we did our usual routine of presents then going to see grandparents. Rocco had not long turned 3 so he thoroughly enjoyed the day, and Revan was 18 months old and was slowly realising the presents were better than the boxes they came in. Christmas day is usually one of the only days I know I can relax, and not focus on work.

After Boxing Day I went back down to Ed's. I asked my oldest son Dennon if he wanted to come and he said he wouldn't mind meeting Ed, so I took him and Tara with me. It was pretty boring for them really, but afterwards Dennon could tell all his friends who he'd met. I got to listen to Ed's new album that was due out in the spring. It was really good - some amazing collaborations on there. Ed then asked if I would like to film for a documentary he was doing for MTV that was coming out in the summer too, so I said I would and to let me know when he would need me. This is why I had a lot of time for Ed: he would always try and help promote me any chance he could. It would be really hard to find somebody who is as genuine as that guy is.

That night the Union J lads had given me a call about getting more work done on their tour and I went to meet them a couple of days later in Nottingham. I always really liked those guys; I had been with them from the beginning of their careers and it was nice to see how far they had come. I only tattooed Jaymi that day as we were running out of time, but we ended up just finishing his sleeve off. In the afternoon their manager popped in to see if we wanted to go meet David Hasselhoff, who was working at a panto in the next building to us. I could not believe it - I fucking loved Knight Rider as a kid! He was a really nice guy and he was asking what it is with British people all getting tattooed. He was a really tall guy too: I'm 6ft4 and he was a lot taller than me. He even had a photo with us all before he had to go on stage: it's always really nice to see when a celeb is like that; it doesn't cost anything to just be nice to people because at the end of the day your fans are what make you famous in the first place.

We went back to the lads' dressing room for a while to wait for the gig to start. Jaymi had made friends with Sam Bailey, the 2013 X Factor winner whilst she was on the show and she was planning on coming up to this gig with her kids and husband. When she got there she came back stage to meet the guys. She was so down-to -earth; it had not changed her at all winning the x factor only a month or so before. She said that she wanted to get the kids some bits from the merchandise stands out front, but the Union J lads' manager offered to go get them what they wanted, so she didn't have to go out with all the fans also waiting to buy stuff. She was having none of it, though. She said she'd just go and wait like everybody else out there. I have got a lot of respect for her doing that. If I'm being totally honest, I don't think I would've done the same.

***

A few days later Celebrity Big Brother started. All the celebs went into the house and when it was Dappy's turn to go on I was doing nothing but hoping and praying they were going to show him for who he really was, and not portray him as the bad guy the media always does. Even as he went in the house he was getting some shit on twitter, and a lot of people were adding me into the tweets because they knew I was his friend. I was getting everything from "Why does he have to talk like a twat?" to, "He is just a chav". But at the end of the day Dappy had come from a poor upbringing like me and made himself one of the best-selling artists in the UK, and every music act I had worked with loved his music. As the weeks went on the hate soon stopped. People were starting to see the real Dappy that I knew - the humble and loving guy he really was.

Meanwhile, I got a call from the guys at Made in Chelsea asking if I would go on the show tattooing them. I said yes, I'd love to do that. We had to sort out a venue, and then get the council to give it the go ahead to tattoo there. There was a lot of fucking around with days and places until Ed Sheeran's record label told me about a place they use sometimes for photo shoots. It was called House of Wolf, a really cool pub in Islington. I had to tattoo Oliver Proudlock a wolf on his arm to cover the Lost Boy that we did in the first place. We did 90 per cent of it before they came to film, leaving the last bits for filming. They wouldn't let Oli talk to the other guys about anything till they started filming. When the programme is filmed they have little chats with them all about what they have been up to. Then the only bit that is set up is the order they have to say it all in. It was so laid back! By far the easiest thing I have ever filmed.

After filming I went looking for trainers. This was still my greatest weakness in life - my love for old, rare trainers. I wanted all the shoes I never had as a kid, and by this time I already had about 50 classic Nikes, mostly Jordans.

***

I ended up spending over £1200 on two pairs I had wanted for a long time. Then I decided to go back to the train station to chill out in the First Class room to wait for my train. I still had an hour or so to wait though, and it was really hot in there so I went and stood outside the room on the chairs there. I was just daydreaming about the day and what I had been doing when this guy came up to me. He must have been in his 50s and he was really smart looking; when he spoke I would say he sounded posh. He asked if I was ok and I was still in a bit of a day dream but I said, "Yes, I'm fine thanks – I'm just waiting for my train." But he kept asking if I was sure I was ok! He was being really nice when he was saying it but he didn't seem to want to believe I really was just waiting, and I was fine. Then he said, "OK, I'm just checking you're alright. Are you homeless?"

I could not believe what he had just said, the cheeky cunt! I was a bit shocked at first, but I had to laugh it off because I could see he was just trying to be nice. Well, I think he was - or he was trying to bum me, but I don't like to think that was the case.

I was in shock when I got on the train: I could not believe what had just happened. I had just spent £1200 on trainers and I was wearing about two grands' worth of stuff. How the fuck could I look like a homeless person? My missus found great joy in it when I told her about it though!

The next day I got a letter from Big Brother again asking if I was interested in going on. It wasn't something I had seen myself doing at all, but it would be a good way to make some big money to get the boys a house of their own. I spoke to Ed Sheeran and Rizzle Kicks about it and they both said I should go for it, so I went for a meeting with them. They wanted me to do the normal Big Brother in the summer. I really didn't like the sound of that, as I was already bigger than half the people who have been in some of the celebrity ones, but for some reason I keep getting pulled back to it. I believe things happen for a reason so I just let it flow and see where it took me.

I had a conversation with the management for some of the lads off the MTV reality shows; we spoke about them looking after me and trying to promote me and we arranged a meeting just outside of Liverpool at one of their houses. One of them was really interested in me doing a clothing range. When we got there it was a massive house in the countryside. They weren't there when I arrived, so I had to wait outside till they came. When they turned up something just seemed dodgy to me, but I thought I would give them a chance to see what they had to say. They were telling me all about the acts they had under them and the money they were already making them. One of them said he was making their main act 700 grand a year just off clothing and he reckoned they would be make me the same kind of money within a year. It all just seemed a bit too good to be true.

They then started to tell me how the industry works and I think this was the point that I lost interest in dealing with them because they didn't have a clue what they were going on about. Everybody I ever meet likes to say that they know Ed Sheeran or that they have managed him, and it's beyond me why they would say it to me. Surely they just don't understand I'm going to ask him. Everything they were saying about people was wrong; they didn't have a clue. It's a real problem with the industry. People say they are big time managers but they just wait for people to be on TV then try and scam them out of money – it's really easy to get gigs for people when their on TV already. They said they could make my company worth 2 million in 2 years and they was really trying to over sell it. Anyway, we left it at that and planned a second meeting a week or so later. I only really agreed on the basis I would give them a check in the meantime and have a little look at the "so called" contract they had written up for me even before I'd agreed to sign it.

We planned a meet at a hotel in Manchester and when I got there I noticed Rizzle Kicks tour bus was outside. I went up to them and asked if the lads were there and they said they would let them know I was about. When they came in they had a chat with me and I told them what I was doing there. Their tour manager said "It's not these guys you're dealing with is it?" giving their names – and it was the people he thought it was. He said to watch them and that they were only club promoters. He was telling me some stories of what they had done to other acts. They never even showed up, so I decided to call it a lucky escape and left. There are so many cowboys out there trying to rip you off and most of the acts don't know any better when they become famous. They hear money bells in their ears and assume they'll be ok.

About a day or so later I got a call from Big Brother to go meet them at a hotel in Manchester - huge pain in the ass, as I had just been in Manchester 2 days before. When I went up there were loads of people desperate to be famous. I recognised a few of them, and I really didn't feel like I fitted in. I was already far past that point in my career, so I decided just to keep my head down.

I soon got rushed in first with some others. We all had to wait in a room and they made us all sit in a line. It was like being back at school and I fucking hated school! We had to play some games and they asked us questions to provoke a response, most of them just gave the safe answers, but I just spoke my mind. You were told to stand in different places depending on your answer and I ended up stood on my own more than once. I had spent two years being told by people to not upset anybody or speak out about things because it could end up deadly for your career, but I was getting sick of it. That's not what I'm like at all, and I really think that's what had held me back for so long.

At the end of it all they asked us what we thought of one person that we didn't want to see go through. There was this little lad who had been to Parliament about tram routes going past his house. He was a real bell end but a nice lad deep down. I just didn't think he would have handled the shit he would've got in the house, so I said I thought he was too much of a pathetic human being to be in a place like that, and he would just be hated. The look of shock smeared across the Big

Brother people's faces at my reply! But I was only saying it in a positive way, to help him.

People really don't understand the effect of being on telly; you get so much hate from nobodies on their phones. It would get the strongest of people down at times. I've always tried to keep my head down as far as possible, but it all gets too much after a while and I try to get a gap month to spend time with the family. Especially now as I might end up doing Big Brother, so every second counted.

***

I had not seen Ray for a while then when he came back up he was telling me about his new manager. He sounded really happy with him, painting a picture of someone who was a big name in the industry, but I had never heard of him. Ray told me he was good friends with Ed Sheeran and that Ed had played at his birthday party. I hear this type of thing about Ed all the time; everybody likes to say they know him when really they mean they have met him. Ray kept asking me to say hi from his manager. I don't normally mention any of it to Ed, though - he really doesn't want to hear it all the time.

As I was talking to Ray I could see a change in him. He used to be all about his wife Emma and making sure she was happy with what he was doing, but it seemed like he didn't care what she thought about him getting tattooed any more. I had a gut feeling about his manager but it was nothing to do with me. Ray was starting to turn his half sleeve into a full one and it was slowly coming together. He was filming Dancing on Ice at the time, and we planned for me to go on the tour with them at some point to try and finish the sleeve.

I had a meeting with Ed Sheeran soon after this about the next bit of his tattoo, and when I was there I thought I would ask him about what Ray had said about his new manager. I asked him if he knew the guy and he said he didn't. I even showed him a photo on his twitter, but he still said he didn't know him. This wasn't surprising because you can normally tell the ones who do know him. If he knew him so well and he had played at his birthday party, would they have not still been in contact, through friends and family? Those who really do know Ed are usually the ones that don't break their necks trying to tell me about it.

I still didn't feel like it was my place to tell Ray. If he was happy with him, that's all that mattered. When I went out on the tour with Ray he did bring it up again, so I just said yes, I would have a word with Ed and started to change what we were talking about. He was telling me his manager made his money from managing Blue back in the day. I knew Blue, so I was sure he didn't manage them at all. I was starting to feel like he was being fed some bull shit by his new manager, but he was still happy with him so I kept my nose out.

That night I stayed on the tour. The wife came up and I took her to see the show. I didn't think it was going to be that good, but I fucking loved it on the night and Joe Pasquale really made the show for me. It was nice to spend some time with the wife too - I had been working so hard.

Chapter 13

I got a text from a lad called Joe Tracini from Hollyoaks; he played someone called Dennis in the show. Tara watches it without fail, which is how I know these things. He was asking about getting a new tattoo - a singing skeleton down his arm. He seemed just like he did on the show, a really bubbly, happy fun chap. I made a plan to go up to his place in Liverpool, where he lived. I thought it would be a posh little gaff he had, but it was a big old building that had been turned into flats. It wasn't in one of the best of parts of Liverpool and he told me that one of the guys who used to be on the show got mugged and beaten up at the top of the road. I was shocked! You wouldn't think people on TV would live like that. When I got there Charlie Wernham, who played Robbie Roscoe on the show, was there as well. They were really nice guys and I ended up tattooing both of them. Joe's was a big piece, but Charlie just had a little one on his ankle. I didn't realise it at first, but Joe's dad was Joe Pasquale; he said that his dad was working with Ray Quinn on the Dancing on Ice tour and as soon as he had told me that I could really see the resemblance.

The kids were starting to grow up fast now and I was working 7 days a week. I hated it. I missed so much of their baby days but I just had to work. After all the press I was getting there were people from all over the world coming to get tattooed by me, flying all the way from Australia, America, everywhere - you name it. I was also getting a lot of millionaires wanting private meetings with me and some of the houses I went in were amazing. I had one guy ask me if I would tattoo his 16 year old daughter for her birthday because she was a massive One Direction fan. I told him I couldn't do anything till she was 18, but people with that much money don't like to hear the word no. He offered me £20,000 to do the tattoo, but I had worked so hard to get a good name and I could've lost it all just by doing that one tattoo. I also didn't think kids of that age should be getting tattooed. I'd done it as a kid and I so much regretted it. As you get older you really do change your mind on what you're into. After everything with the talks in schools I'd done last year for tattoo regulations I wasn't prepared to do anything for no matter what amount of money.

Don't get me wrong, I could've cried turning that amount of money down. I have never made a mass amount from tattooing as I never put my prices up after this all kicked off. I didn't want to cut off all my normal clients just because I was doing some celebrity tattooing. It was mad, as the only reason I started doing them was to charge more, but I was in a place by then where I could be a bit choosier with what I was doing.

I've loved drawing all my life, but all I was doing now was shitty little things I didn't even like. It had all become about making big money for the boys. I couldn't see that I was going to end up doing any bigger than Harry or Ed anyway. People just didn't care anymore; they all thought I tattooed all and sundry anyway. Life was just getting mental for me: It was non-stop. I was tuning in to features about the 'Tattooist to the Rich and Famous' and every newspaper or TV show I did would introduce me as the 'Celebrity Tattooist', a tag which didn't take long to stick, but I wanted to keep it real still.

I was sat at home one night and I got a text asking if I had seen what James Arthur had been putting on twitter. I don't ever really check what people put on there, but I had a look to see what it was. Apparently he'd put that he'd had a fall out with some guy on there who was bitching about him, and he'd made some comment about being queer. He wasn't - it was just a silly comment he made in the heat of the moment. James is a nice guy deep down; I just thought he found it hard being famous. He got bad panic attacks sometimes and of course I could understand how he felt with that, so being famous would just make it that much worse. When I saw what he'd put I tried to get hold of him but couldn't get a reply.

The next day I had to do an interview for one of the papers about something I was doing. At the end of the interview they asked me what I thought of what James had said. I just told them that it had all been blown out of proportion, and he was not homophobic at all. There was another act trying to make things worse for

James on twitter, and I could tell they were just doing it to try and promote themselves. I told the paper he was a nice lad and it was all getting out of hand over one silly comment. Within an hour the paper had my comments on line; they never ran any of the rest of the story - they were just asking for reactions to my comments about James. I got so much hate from the public on twitter over it; from mad people calling me homophobic. I never really pay much attention to haters on the net though. Usually within a day or two people soon move on and hate somebody else.

***

One huge problem I found in the music industry was the amount that some of them smoked weed. It made them so paranoid all the time. There are two acts I can think of who have had a big problem with weed. They would get stoned most nights, and after taking it for a while it makes people very panicky. But then they take more to try to stop the panic feeling. It's a never-ending problem. I have tried to talk sense into them with my past experience, but they just don't want to know.

I had spent so much time in the music industry over the last couple of years that I now knew how it all worked, and I would get asked by some of the acts if I would help link them with people, or even get them press. My name has been used by some big acts just to make up a story to help sell records. It was mental – I'm just a tattooist - but I was mixing with a big league and getting in the papers all the time. By now I wasn't getting any happiness from what I do, so helping others was how I got my kicks. I had one act tell me he couldn't get the papers to run any stories about him at all. I took that as a challenge and within a week I got a story printed about them. When I showed it to him he was really pissed off; he said he pays his management loads of money and they could never do what I did in a week. He asked me if I would work for him, and the idea of managing acts is interesting to me, but I was on a good thing with what I did already. I would never equal that as a manager, except maybe when I'm older. The Made in Chelsea thing aired and everyone was going mental booking in and telling me they had just seen me on the TV and I had more and more people noticing me in the streets. That's not too bad, as I never really get stopped; people just double take and you can hear them say, "That's him that does so-and-so's tattoo!" I just smile to myself when I hear them as I go past.

I got asked to go to a VIP party in London – the kind of thing I didn't really like. I had to spend so much time away from home that if I wasn't working I just wanted to be at home with Tara and the boys, but I had to turn up to some of them, just to keep my face out there. I always find it odd that clubs of that type really only ever let in the really rich or famous guys. You would always see footballers there, and the only girls that seemed to be allowed in were the gold digger types. You could see they spent every second of everyday just making themselves look good just to try pull a rich guy in a club.

There were a lot of celebs in there that night half of them I already knew. At the end of the night I saw a well-known female act leaving the club with a footballer she was seeing. She was off her tits on something - she didn't know what day it was - you could see the footballer didn't give a fuck about her. She had white powder around her nose and a friend of mine who looks after some of the acts I have worked with pulled her to one side and cleaned her up before she could leave. There were paparazzi everywhere just waiting for people to leave the club, and it wouldn't have been good for her career if he hadn't cleaned her up before she left.

***

Shortly after this I got offered to do Soccer Six again and I was a little sceptical at first after last year's one. Tara wasn't allowed anywhere near me, but all the bigger, better-known celebrities partners and plus ones were allowed on the pitch with them. I told the guy that owns it that I'd only do it on condition that Tara had the same pass as me. He agreed, and the night before me and Tara went out in London for food with Joe Tracini, We were in Leicester Square in some bar that looked down on the square itself, and it was a lovely night. We drove down the next morning and it turned out ok, even though my team didn't come anywhere near as good as we had last year.

Tara was stood with James Arthur's manager and then girlfriend. There are always a few celebs that do the Soccer Six matches and think they are a million times better than everyone else, in reality they are on exactly the same level!

It was getting closer to my birthday and Big Brother still hadn't been in touch. They had given me all the signs that I was going to be in, but they just leave you hanging. I was telling Ed about it all and he said he thought it would be a good idea to do, as it would help build my portfolio with the British public. I still wasn't that keen but just went along with it and one night Ed tweeted them direct saying, "Can't wait to see Kevin Paul in the Big Brother house!"

I didn't know he had done it until my phone went mental, and his comment got retweeted about 4000 times in a matter of days. I had press keep calling asking about it and I just had to say no, which just made things worse as people started saying I must be in the celebrity one, and then everybody started repeating that. In the end I had to leave the country till people moved on to the next story. I have always loved the TV show *Benidorm* and watch it every time a new series starts, so I thought fuck - it lets go there! I don't really like tacky Spain holidays, but I really loved it there. It was a nice hotel, really quiet and out the way and we found a lovely place called Yorkshire Pride to have food every day. Even the boys loved it. It was a really nice break and I was making the most of not having to get up with an alarm every morning. The night Big Brother started we were walking down by the beach and my phone was going nuts. Everybody thought because I was away I must have been in hiding and I was getting friends and celebs texting to see if I was in. Looking back at it, I'm so happy I didn't do it, as it was so shit - a bunch of nobodies with nothing worth saying.

When we got back I had to work as hard as I could to make up for having a week off of work. Ed's documentary then aired on MTV and was shown worldwide I think. It was really good: it showed you where he grew up, and he was saying how he went from busking to filling out arenas. I wasn't on it for long, but people knew who I was and were sending photos saying, "You're on my TV again, *Kevin Paul*."

***

A few weeks past of mainly doing local people and then Dappy got in touch again. Whenever he came up he liked to go in the Westfield Shopping Centre; there was a place that did Greek food and he loved it there but every single time we went in we got mobbed by fans. We had to go out the back of a shop one day because there were so many people trying to get to him. It was mental! We got back to the car and made our way back to the studio, but then we pulled up at some traffic lights and Dappy saw a girl he liked the look of; he tried to get her attention and it didn't take long before he did. He kept asking her to come down the studio, and you could see she really did want to; the only problem was she was sat next to her boyfriend in the car. Dappy was unstoppable when it came down to women, but he was always nice to everybody. You could see he just wanted to please everybody all the time. I know about all the shit the papers say he did, but I know the facts about it too, and it really wasn't like the way it was printed.

We managed to more or less finish up his arm, although whenever he's in the chair, he's like a child in a sweet shop, wanting everything!

***

It was the middle of summer: Rocco was ready for pre-school soon, and I wanted to move somewhere nice to send him to school. I had not long tattooed a teacher from a village called Melbourne, just next to Donington Park; I knew the place already as I use to go to the market out there when I was younger. This teacher was telling me how good the school was and how everybody in the village all helped each other. It was just what I wanted for the boys; it was so like where Ed was brought up. So the next day I tried to go see some places, but every one that we found had gone within a day; I could see it was going to be harder than I first thought.

This went on for about a month, and then Tara saw a house come up. It was only small so we were sceptical about viewing it but we did, just in case, and at least we would be in the village at last. Tara arranged a viewing and it was surprisingly bigger than the pictures made it look. I told her to just take it, so she phoned them straight away and paid a deposit on it. We still had 3 months left on the house we were already in which meant I had to pay for both houses until it was over. It nearly broke me at the time, but it was so worth it! It's such a beautiful place to live, and it makes everything I have ever done worth every last penny. Everybody would say how well I had done, but at the end of the day we were still renting the house, so I didn't feel like I had done anything. Maybe I would feel different if I had the money to *buy* a home for my boys, but until that day it didn't mean anything to me what people said. I have always had a low opinion of myself anyway. After we moved in I got a call from a TV production company about me doing a tattoo programme. It was going to be on E4. I didn't really know how I felt about it, as I had already helped on loads of other shows and been a specialist for one about fixing up bad tattoos, but I went with it to see where it would go. I liked the sound of what they were saying, but most stuff like this doesn't ever end up making it to the TV screen. Then I found out one of the guys from London Ink was going to be on it, and this was a big no no for me. I didn't want anything to do with that shit, and after that I lost any interest in doing it. To be honest I was losing interest in doing any more TV things at all. I knew I had made a brand out of myself, but I just didn't know what way to take it.

Round about then I got a call from a movie producer I had met the year before. He wanted a meet in London about a film he was doing. It was a film about his life involved with the underworld of gangsters and how he would move his money around by putting it in to making films. It sounded like a really good film, and he asked me if I would like to play a part in it. I have never been an actor or wanted to be, but I thought yes, I'm up for that! He was telling me about how it all came together and how he started by making it in to a book, and the more I thought about it, I thought my life was not much different to his. Maybe I should do a book too. I sent his publisher an email telling them all about me and my life and I went to meet them a couple of weeks later in London.

Clifford and Ruth seemed a really nice couple. They come across really posh - not the sort of people I would normally come across in life, but they seemed like they could do what they said they could do. It made me smile that I would be mentioning stars such as Ed Sheeran and they didn't know who I was talking about. Clifford later told me he thought Ed was some old footballer. I always keep an open mind at first to see how things pan out; you meet so many people in this game who are full of shit or say they have done stuff they have not done but I ended up signing a deal with them to do this book.

***

Rocco had just started pre-school and it was so nice to hear him talk about his little friend he had made at school. Shortly after that we arranged for Revan to go, even though he wasn't 3 yet. He was crying for his brother while he was at school, but now they get to go together and it's so nice. I come in from work and they tell me all about their day. This is what I'm doing everything for - for them.

A few weeks later just before Rocco's 4th birthday I saw on instagram that Paul Booth, the tattooist I'd loved from the start of my tattooing career, was coming back to the UK for the first time in ten years. I had to try and get a booking with him, and I tried everything to get hold of him - twitter, email, I even contacted Danni Filth from Cradle of Filth, but got no joy. Then I remembered that Lal Hardy I used to work with knew him well, and he would be working at his before the show he was doing over here. I dropped him a text about it and he got back to me really fast, saying yes, not a problem. I'm sure Paul would sort it. I was so happy! It had been a big dream of mine to get tattooed by him for so many years, and I really owe Lal so much for making it happen. When I got there he was really nice. He didn't say much - you could see he was in work mode - but that's why he is so good at what he does. I didn't think he would get much done, but when he started drawing it went all over my side, and it looks amazing. He did an evil hand with his trademark leaf effect thing coming off I; it hurt like hell and took around 7 hours but it was worth every second. This was not just a tattoo to me: it meant so much more. He told me I was welcome to come over to New York to his studio whenever I wanted. I could not wait to get more done on it by him.

***

Clifford and Ruth had told me about a book festival in the Isle of Wight where they had set up a stand for us all. To be honest it was really shit and a total waste of my time, but they paid for us to be there and it was good to meet their other authors. Afterwards we all went for a meal at the hotel. I could see they was really gutted it hadn't go so well, but I could see their hearts were fully into it and really wanted all there authors to do well. From that point on I knew I could trust them. It was just coming up to the end of 2014 at this point, and I was about to go on my last two tours of 2014. Ed Sheeran's and the Big Boy Band reunion tour. I remembered Tara saying that growing up she loved Blue and Five, so I knew she would want to come along. It may seem like I have a cool life style mixing with all the celebs when you see it on twitter or in the papers, but trust me, it's hard work.

I got up about 6 on the Monday morning to go see Ed. I was looking forward to it, as I hadn't seen him for a while and it was nice to catch up. We had are normal dinner before we got cracking on trying to finish the top of his sleeve. We had a good 4 hours on it, but then we then had to get over to the gig in Birmingham. When he got there he had an interview lined up with Dan Wootton from the Sun newspaper. I knew who he was, as he goes on Daybreak in the morning reporting on anything celebrity and runs the celeb section of the Sun, he was about as big as it gets for UK celeb press. He seemed a nice guy, very friendly. I'd heard of him before from other acts, and I knew a lot of people were scared of his stories coming out – apparently he could make you or break you.

After he finished his interview with Ed I got to have a chat with him and he seemed to take an interest in what I did; he even had a photo with me for twitter so we could make out he was getting tattooed. When Ed went out on to the stage I went out with him and I couldn't believe how loud the crowd went up - it was insane! I left soon after. I always liked Ed's tours as it's like one big family; everybody helps each other and his door is always open to everybody. I have never been on a tour like it.

The next morning I was back at the hotel but this time it was with the Big Boy Band Reunion Tour. Ed was still in the hotel and I had told Scott Robinson from Five that I would take him to meet him, as he was such a big fan. So I took him and I told him no kissing his arse or asking him to sing a song with you! Joking with him as I knew he wanted to ask him but when he met him he was so nice, he was telling Ed how he had been big all those years ago, and how lucky he was to get a second chance. It was a nice morning and Ed really seemed interested in what he had to say. Then Scott had a call then from Lee Ryan from Blue, who also wanted to come meet Ed. I didn't know how he would be, as he can be a live wire at times, but he was so polite and you could see he was really trying not to swear - it was funny to watch.

Later that day I went and tattooed Scott back at the place I was with Ed at the night before: it was odd, as it was the same place but everything was different. I had already been and met everybody a couple of days before, so I knew my way around with them all. I got going as soon as I could as I was back out with Ed the next day in Nottingham.

When I got there he was still in bed so I just went for a drink with his management. When we finally went up to his room it was so cool, like a little posh cottage. It even had a piano in there, which was odd as it was really the top floor of a hotel in the middle of Nottingham. We ordered in Nandos, as we normally did to start off a long day and then we got cracking on his sleeve. We must have done a good 4 hours again - he was hardcore when he got going with his tattoos!

When we got done I went down to the gig with Ed and his team and we sat watching a TV show from Ireland called *Love Hate*. I think Ed really got into it when he was touring over there; I couldn't watch it properly as I was working, but I still got into it. It was really dark, all about drugs and crime over in Ireland.

Ed's tours always put on the best of foods in the canteen - it was like a big Xmas dinner. Later that night Tara was coming down to watch the gig with some friends. She hadn't seen Ed for a while now, as she was always with the kids, but they were at school now so it was nice for her to catch up with him to. She misses out a lot on what I do now, what with having the kids. It was the first time I had seen the tour this year, and I had heard the album so many times over the last year before it came out, it was nice to finally see him singing it. There is a song on it where he raps, and on stage he starts by tapping the guitar to create a beat; he then sticks it on a loop pedal that keeps the beat going, then he starts his little rap bit. It was really good to watch - I don't usually watch the shows, as I'm linked to them more on the personal side of their lives, not the work part. That was the last time I saw Ed in 2014. We would normally meet up over Xmas at his big house, so I thought that would be it till then.

The next morning my phone was going mental. Dan Wootton's story had come out in the paper, and he'd had put a big bit about me and Ed being good friends and what he had been up to he was nice guy. He didn't have to put anything about me in there at all.

Chapter 14

About a week later I was invited back to the porn awards. We took some friends with us that time too. They couldn't believe what it was like – it's a funny thing to witness. It's mainly full of punters, as well as a bunch of rich men who have paid to be there on the night. My table was in between two porn stars' tables and I spent about 3 hours with a face full of minge and arse holes pushed in my face. I was shocked that some of them where actual porn stars they looked like such nice, clean-living girls and I couldn't believe it when one of them stood up to get an award for best newcomer.

Not long after all this I started to watch a documentary on Channel 4 about a guy who catches out men trying to have sex with kids. I had big respect for him from day one. I even tweeted showing support a couple of days later; he was called Stinson Hunter. I knew the shit he would be getting that night after being on TV after going through it myself with the tattoo regs stuff. You get a lot of support but you always get some dicks that want to hate you - and boy, they *really* fucking hate you! I knew if I was looking after him I could've done big things with him. Over the years I have met so many people in the industry. A lot of people don't understand the deals I'm doing behind the scenes, linking people together and setting up stories for the papers. It was all going on: I was even used in some of the stories myself.

While all this was going on I was trying to move studios too. I had employed some more people to work with me, so that if I'm ever away on meetings the shop is still taking in money. It also meant I could be with my family more. It was stressful, but we finally got there. The new studio is much bigger for us all to work in and yet still relatively private for when I have the odd client that likes their privacy.

***

I got asked to go out on a PA one night with an act from a reality show. A PA is a personal appearance in a club, and it's how most reality stars make their money. They don't really make much money from doing the actual shows, but just being on them makes them worth money to people. When we got there it was full of girls waiting to see them. When you do these types of events the club will always offer the act a rider on top of the money they get paid. You can really try and push your luck with it and see what you can get away with. Most just ask for 1000 fags and champagne. The lads I was with asked for cocaine and vodka. They also got given a room backstage to take girls back to. This was a normal thing to happen at nights like this. Reality shows like they were on tell them to play, get drunk and fuck girls... this makes good TV.

When they started to let people in it was mostly girls in there, and all of them were dripping at the thought of sitting on the faces of the acts I was with. Every last one of them was trying to get their attention. One of the guys was talking to these two blondes and they were only young looking - I would say 17 or 18. After about 20 minutes he took them in the back room and they were gone for over an hour: it was clear what they had been doing, and when he came back out he had video recorded what they had been up to. He had them touching each other before he got them to suck his dick. They were taking it in turns for about 10 minutes before he shot his load over one of their mouths. He got them to kiss afterwards, one with his load still in her mouth then the other one swallowed it. They were really dirty bitches. After they came out we didn't really see them again; I think they got what they'd come for.

One of the girls also videoed some of what went on and about a week later the guy who had been with the girls got an email from the TV production company he worked for. They said they'd had a complaint from one of the girl's dads, and it turned out they were only 15. Strictly speaking, I don't think the act was in the wrong; they really did look at least 18 and the club should have of checked their ID.

The production company ended up by paying off the girl's family to make it all go away. But after all, they tell their acts to fuck girls and get pissed when they're out to make good TV! I was told this type of thing happened all the time - I'm so glad I have sons.

I went out for a meal with my book publishers Clifford and Ruth just before the Xmas rush. We were having a chat about the whole Ray and his management thing. They didn't trust his manager either, but they had just done a book deal with Ray so they had to work with him. Ray was doing a tour over the New Year for his new album and his manager had told them it was going to be a hundred thousand ticket deal. I have been on a lot of tours, and I know what a hundred thousand ticket gig looks like: Ray was not one of them. They were told by him to order books to sell at gigs, but I knew it would be more like ten thousand tickets. Luckily they hadn't ordered that many books; they didn't trust his manager about the stuff he was saying. Ruth said she didn't believe he had really managed Blue, so I said let's find out, and texted Lee Ryan about it all. I asked if this guy had ever managed them, and he replied within minutes, saying no and he was a cunt. I showed them both the text and I think we could all see now that he hadn't done the things he said he had. They thought I should have a word with Ray, but I still didn't think it was my place to do so when he seemed happy with his set up.

***

When Ray came to the studio next he brought up the Ed Sheeran thing again, asking me to say hi from his manager. Eventually I told him Ed had said he didn't know him. He looked a bit shocked and just said, "That's odd - but he did manage Blue!" I didn't have the heart to tell him the truth. I had a lot of time for Ray, he really was a sweet guy; I was just shocked how little he knew about the industry. He really needed to keep his guard up more.

I got a phone call from the guys at Big Brother. The celebrity one was just about to start and they asked me if I would go down and be on Big Brother's Little Brother. It wasn't my type of thing really, but I went down anyway, and I took Tara with me. She had never been on TV before, so it was going to be good to see how she was with it.

When we got there we had to stand around outside with the other people who were going on the show. I really was not used to being on this side of things; I normally go straight back stage and get triple A passes. I didn't like doing things like the general public did and I was getting a bad feeling about the whole thing.

When we got in we had to go sit in a room and watch the show there before we went to the live studio for filming. They pulled me to one side on my way in. About a week before I'd had to send in what I was thinking about the people in the house that year; what I don't think they understood was I had dealings with 3 of the house mates in there, and I knew a lot of dirt on half of them. They had shown the producers my email and I was told I could not say anything when I got in there. They said I knew too much about the house mates and it could turn into a legal matter. In that case, I couldn't really see the point in me being there! I didn't like being treated like a nobody after getting special treatment for so many years. I know I'm not a celeb, but I knew a damn sight more than half the guys in there and I could've fucked their shit right up if I was in that house.

When we went on they wanted us all to wear stupid fucking party hats and dance around! When Rylan came out he didn't say a word to me when he spotted me there. I do understand he might forget some faces, but you don't forget me - I stand out to much. It's funny how it's always the ones that don't do that well that get up themselves. I was really not up one bit for any of this: it was an experience but I wouldn't do it again; I've about had my fill of that show for one life-time!

That night I got a text about one in the morning. It was a guy out of a well-known pop band I had worked with before and he asked me if I could get Ed Sheeran to follow him on twitter. I still find it so mad that big pop stars feel the need to ask me to get him to follow them – that's what their managers are for. It's the only problem with knowing Ed, everybody wants something from him. I have had everything from can I get tickets to his gigs, to will he play at my wedding.

I was asked to go down to London to meet up with one of the acts I have tattooed and has become good friends with me. I'd known him and his family for about 2 years by that point. He was always close to his missus and kid, but I could see something was changing and his music was not doing too well. He was always known as a nice guy, but nice don't cut it in the music world. His management was telling him to spice things up, and that he needed to be seen being more of a bad boy. Of course, this is what sells records. I know it's not nice, but that's the truth. His missus didn't like him doing anything like that; she wanted him to stay like he was, but she didn't understand the world he was in and I did. I had been asked to do a sex tape with a reality show star to try and build press interest, or go to clubs with glamour models, but I would not do anything like that: I love my family and they always come first in my eyes. I could see that this guy was really thinking about leaving his family to make his music work; it was so sad and I felt so sorry for his missus and kids.

I really hated the whole celebrity world I was in, there really was not much good in it at all. They were planning nights out for him in London with some hot models, just to try get some bad stories in the papers to try and make him more popular, and his poor missus would have to read all about this in the papers the next day. I could never do that to my family. I had an act once who picked going to record a new track over being at his kid's birthday. I already hate not being around for my boys much and I could never be like that and put my kids second – it would just fuck them up for when they grow up. A child growing up needs a mum and dad, and to be shown love by both of them.

I don't know why it was but 2015 felt like it was going to be my year. I had film bits coming up and also the book: I knew the book was going to be big because of what's in it.

I have worked on my own for years but I knew it was time to get a bigger place and get more people in working for me. I ended up finding a nice little place by the train station in Derby and now everything was starting to look up. I got a phone call on the Wednesday from a film company asking if I wanted to be in a film. I didn't know much about it, but it sounded good, and so I said I would be happy to do it. They wanted me to film on the Friday, so I had to move all my bookings around in the shop to be able to make it down. They called me that night to tell me more about it; it turned out they wanted me to play a prisoner. I was well up for that - if I was going to do films, I wanted it to be dark and gritty stuff I did.

We were filming at an old prison in Richmond Park, South London. I got there about 8 in the morning, and it was freezing. The first person I bumped into was Sam Strike, who had played Danny Dyer's son in East Enders; he seemed a nice lad and happy to talk.

When I went in it was a bit odd! There were loads of people dressed like police officers. I knew they weren't, but when you see people like that you can't help but think it's real. They gave me a prison uniform to wear: it was some grey joggers and a thin t- shirt, and I was freezing my tits off. They called me on set not long after, but by then I was starting to get a bit nervous about it all. I didn't have a clue what I was doing, or if I could even do it.

They asked me to stand outside a cell door as they were doing a shot along the cells with everybody stood outside their door before it got to the lead actor. They ended up asking me to bend down a bit, as I was too tall for the shot. It was so cold in there and we had to stand around for about 3 hours; I could see my own breath.

After dinner we did the second scene - a riot scene running down the cells. There were about 20 of us running down at the camera man, and I had so much fun I just wanted to do it again. I'd fallen in love with acting right from the first, and I just wanted to do more. When they asked me if I could film again the next day I really wanted to, but I had too much going on at the studio.

I spoke to one of the guys in the production team about my book, and he said I should maybe look at turning it into a film. I had never thought about it before and at first I didn't see that I was that big a deal but the more I thought about it, the more I could see it might actually work. Anyway, we swopped details and I got on my way back to the Midlands.

I loved it I just wanted to do more acting work from that moment on. But don't get me wrong, it was so much hard work, not I liked sitting in my little warm studio drawing on people. I couldn't get it out of my head about doing a film - I'd had a real light bulb moment, just like when I wanted to do the celebrity tattooing thing, and look what happened there! Everything was going so well I just could not help thinking that something had to go wrong soon.

***

My babies were happy in the county side and at a good school, work was going well and branching out into new, bigger things, and I couldn't wait to see what was going to happen next. My publisher had told me my ex-wife was actually trying to sue them if we put anything about her in the book! (I knew she would do something like that - she is mental.) She said she didn't want the staff at her work finding out about what she'd got up to: you would think her new fella would wonder why she is so bothered about what was in the book. For me it was about setting down the facts about how I got to where I am and what really happened along the way. I was getting sick of half facts and the shit the papers had run about me and Harry Styles. This book tells it all in my own words. I also wanted people to see that no matter where you came from or what education you have, you can make something of yourself. Don't listen to anybody putting you down - keep your head up strong and go for it!

Over the last two years I have put loads of the people I have worked with in touch with each other, and this has led to them recording songs together and much more. I have learnt how the press works and how to make good money from it all and I loved setting fake stories up about a celebrity and some unknown girl having a so-called affair, when really they have just been seen together for a photo - simply to help that act get a top ten record. It really is shocking how dumb the British public can be! I could see I could really make some money from it all.

Some of the acts I worked with asked me if I could help them with stories, or make them more popular. I couldn't understand why their own management couldn't do it themselves. I found it so easy with all the contacts I had made to get stories about anybody or anything. I didn't really see myself as a tattooist any more; of course, I *was* still a tattooist and that's where I made my money, but I wanted to move on to other things. I had been offered a part in two films. I knew I was never going to be a real actor, but I can do nasty better than most – after all, end of the day I have really lived it!

I didn't know exactly what I wanted to do next, but I knew I was going to stay in the entertainment game. The more and more I thought about it I decided to do PR and manage the acts. I had already been doing half of their stuff already - I just never made any money from it.

There are a lot of dodgy tattooists out there claiming to be 'celebrity tattooists' because they did some nobody off some shit reality show 4 years ago. No! That doesn't make you a celebrity tattooist at all. What does is being part of their life and mixing with them out of hours; helping get the press for them and linking them with gigs. I've been getting Soccer Six some of its top acts for the last two years, but people just don't see that side of my work. 2015 is going to be the year I stand up and speak my mind. I have spent 3 years being told what I can and can't say on TV and in the media. Fuck that! This year you will hear the truth about what I really think.

Chapter 15

Ray asked me to go down to tattoo him and his manager; I didn't really want to do this, but I could see changes in Ray. I said to Tara before I went down that I thought he would split with his missus, and I knew what he would want to talk about. When I got there Ray's manager seemed a nice guy, and as soon as I sat down with him he started to tell me how well he knew Ed Sheeran. I didn't want to hear it - I really didn't care if he did or didn't know him – so I just kept changing what we talked about.

He started to tell me about knowing Blue, so I said yes, I know them too. He asked how I knew them and when I said I had been on tour with them he looked a bit shocked that I knew them that well. He soon shut up going on about them, he just reckoned that they didn't get on, so he dropped them. I knew he was talking shit but saying all this, he still seemed a nice guy. He even paid for my hotel down there.

Ray was telling me about him and his missus, saying it was not the same any more. She was finding it hard with him being away all the time and I could see he wanted to end it - he was just scared about losing contact to his son. I told him all about when I split up with my oldest son's mum. I could see it was really cutting him up about what to do with it all. His manager obviously didn't like her, and he was always getting at Ray to fuck her off. It was wrong - he should've left him to sort it out himself. I could tell he was just trying to keep Ray away from everybody else in his life, but Ray couldn't see it.

Ray asked me to pop back down to try and finish his arm, and said his manager wanted to get a little tattoo done too. I didn't mind so much this time, as he was ok the last time I popped down. Ray was still in bits about his missus and what to do about it all and I could see it was just a matter of time before they split. I told him when he did to let me know. I had a lot of press contacts and it needed to be handled right in the papers. I even told them what to say.

***

Clifford called me on a Sunday afternoon and told me while he had been drinking with Ray and his manager he'd asked him if he knew Ed Sheeran, as he had been told that Ed did not know him and he did not even recognise a picture of him. Ray's manager had a little hissy fit, shouting and having a go. When I put the phone down I got a text off his manager saying he didn't know why I'd said that, and he just kept going on about how he *did* know Ed. I didn't give a fuck I told him. Then he dropped his attitude, wanting to know if we were still friends. I told him we were never not friends - I just didn't want to know.

About two days later he called me saying Ray had split

with his missus and was really cut up about it all. He asked me what I thought he should do, so I told him what to say to the papers about it all, and how to go about it. I found it funny that this guy was saying he was such a big manager but he was asking a tattooist what to do. Anyway, I gave it a day or two and still nothing had come out about it all. I asked him what was going on, but he just said it was all in hand.

About a week later I was told Ray's manager was going to release publicity for Ray's tour and he was going to have a bitch at the industry because they wouldn't play Ray's music. This is definitely not the type of thing you should do! He also wanted to release about the split with Ray and his wife, despite what I'd told them. The next day it all came out in the papers, and it was so bad what his manager put. He just tried to make it all about the music by talking about how sad Ray was about the split. He made Ray look so bad and Ray is nothing like that. He is such a sweet guy and he loves his son so much - anybody could see that. Dan Wooton at the Sun commented on what his manager put out, and I knew Dan so I tried to tell him this was not Ray, it was his dick of a manager. I told him everything about what a cock this guy was and how Ray had been taken in by it. All that morning the Sun had run a little bit about Ray in a bad light after the press release his manager did.

The next day Ray was in the final of a show on ITV. Ray's manager didn't go with him to the studio that day. He stayed at home and put out a big bitch about Dan Wooton for what was said. It was really bad - he even threatened him – and it showed how unprofessional he was. I knew Dan had seen it, as he asked me about who he was. I told him all the facts about what had gone on; I just didn't want this back-firing on Ray. I couldn't speak to Ray as he was filming and he didn't know anything about it all.

Then about an hour later his manager put up a video slagging Dan off again. He made nasty comments about him being gay and told him to watch himself around London. I could not believe what I was hearing - I had to put a stop to this. I made sure Dan knew this was nothing to do with Ray, and I dropped Ray a text telling him all about it for when he came off air. Ray ended up winning the show and I could not believe how good it was. His manager was damaging it all for him, and the next morning I just had to tell Ray the facts about everything I knew. He really needed to get away from this guy before he fucked up his whole career. When I spoke to him he seemed to know what I was saying was true.

On the Monday morning after he won the ITV Show 'Get Your Act Together' I spoke to him about the events of the weekend. There was no way he could stay with his manager as his career would be over. After winning a prime time show on ITV you would expect to be asked to appear on the popular day time TV shows the following week, but Ray got offered nothing and there was also no press.

I told him he needed to get out of this situation. His manager had lied to him about who he was and what influence he had in the industry, but Ray said if he walked away from this he would have nothing. I told him he would be alright, I would help him get it all sorted. I also advised him to contact Clifford at his publishers and speak to him.

Clifford called me early in the afternoon and asked me if I knew that Ray was in a bad way; he had spoken to Ray and his mum and dad and offered Ray his spare room at his house, as Ray wanted some time away from his manager. At the time Ray was living in the pub that his manager owned.

***

That afternoon I had a long discussion with Clifford about what was going to happen to Ray and his upcoming gigs. Ray and his mum and dad had gone to Clifford's house and discussed what the situation was. Clifford also had a meeting with Ray's producers that night as now the word was out that there had been a split between Ray and his manager. The tour and the new album were up in the air.

Clifford was not just a publisher, he also other business interests and in his younger days had run club nights and managed some unsigned bands, so he knew how to handle a tour. The phone was off the hook for the next few days, with Clifford organising the gigs, meeting the producers of the new album and looking after Ray. I was calling all my contacts at ITV, Luke Williams about managing Ray, and organising Ray to join my campaign for safe tattooing.

A meeting had been set up to meet MP Chris Williamson in Parliament, which Ray came along to. The funny thing was while I was waiting to meet up with Ray, Clifford, my apprentice Lucy and me got pulled by the Old Bill for looking dodgy while walking around the outside of the Houses of Parliament. Unbeknown to me in a few hours' time I would be walking around the *inside!* The meeting had already been set up, as Clifford was helping me by using a contact he had who was a political adviser. Ray was in the meeting too, and it was then filmed as part of a Channel Five TV documentary.

Ray was still looking a bit shell-shocked. We were taken on a tour around Parliament and through some secret tunnels by Clifford's associate, and passed all the security. It was cool, like the set of a Harry Potter movie, but Ray still looked in a bit of a daze. You could tell this week had been a shock for him. I had Channel 5 filming me that day for the tattoo bill and they were more than happy to have Ray involved. Then that afternoon he was off to having a meeting with Clifford's lawyers.

Later on I met them at King's Cross where we had a meeting with Ray's producers Troika Studios. The guys seemed really concerned about Ray; they seemed to really like Ray and believe in his work, which was a good start. Sam Ellis was a very stern guy, and I sat there and listened to what they all had to say. I got the feeling that they had Ray's best interests at heart and to me this is what Ray needed.

Clifford stayed with Ray and I left to go back to Derby with Lucy Hilbert, who is my apprentice but also works with Clifford doing all the PR leg work for his companies.

I sat with Lucy and discussed with her what the next plans for Ray would be. I said he needed high profile TV, 'A Night with Ray Quinn' or something like that.

I got Lucy to contact ITV, and within a week they had got back to her, and Clifford had been asked to come into ITV to meet some executive producers who wanted to pitch some ideas to them.

Clifford had now taken over as interim manager of Ray and was looking after his tour and business interests. We were all looking to find a decent music management guy to look after Ray as well. Clifford had been dealing with the producers at Troika Studios to sort out the legal details of Ray's new album. Within the details, Clifford had set up Phoenix Records UK Ltd of which Ray was 100% shareholder and director. The idea was that Ray would be in full control of his album and licences. Clifford had taken him under his wing and after working with him for three months on his book, had learnt a lot about Ray and where he had gone wrong in his career. Clifford approached me and asked if I would like to get involved with the setting up of a label. We had all the contacts - a producer, music management contacts - so why not.

Ray came to my studio to have his tattoos finished and Channel 5 was there to film us at the studio. This was good for both of us. I also got Ray on local radio and I appeared in a number of local papers.

***

Ray seemed a lot happier now and more confident in himself. He joked about how strict Clifford and Ruth are with him and that they don't allow him to have his phone when he goes to bed. When he asked them where his phone was because it needed charging, they told him it was in the oven!

That Wednesday Ray did his first book signing and gig with his new team, which I am proud to part of, and it was a great success. I am confident that going forward with this group of people around me, there are bigger and better things on the horizon.

I feel relieved that I have survived and even triumphed on this journey through 'trouble to notoriety', and that it will not be long before I am able to give my two sons the life I always wanted for myself, private schooling and a house of our own.

Thanks

I want to give a big thanks to Andy Meakin and Loughborough Uni for making any of this possible in the first place by letting me meet the celebrity acts who have performed at the uni over the past 4 years. I owe you and Evo big time for it. None of it would ever have happened without your faith in me from the start. I also want to thank Andy P. - you know who you are! – for showing me how the music industry works and how to deal with the press. I feel like I owe you so much for all your help back when I started in this game.

Thank you to the Rizzle Kicks boys for giving me a shot in the first place and letting me tattoo you. Your support give me the break I needed, and I also want to thank you for linking me with Ed Sheeran - that guy changed my life.

Massive thanks to Ed Sheeran himself. I can only hope my kids turn out to be half as nice as you. If they do I will be a proud parent because you're a true gent and one of the nicest guys I have ever met. You have done so much for me and my family over the years, and you don't even know it! I have big love for you Dude, and I will always have your back.

I want to thank Dappy for all his support too. You're a pain in the arse, but I do love you, Dude! And many thanks to Mark at Soccer Six for all his support over the last 2 years, and for letting me play in the game.

Special thanks to Andy Collier from Andy's Tattoo Studio in Burton on Trent for getting me started in the game from a young age. I still have good memories of it all.

Last but by no means least, I want to thank my beautiful wife for giving me my two beautiful boys Rocco and Revan. They are my everything and my reason to succeed in life, and I am so grateful for all your support over the last 4 years while I have been working 7 days a week, every hour God sends to try and make a better life for my boys.

More Titles from
Percy Publishing Fiction

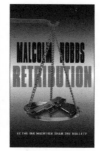

The Middle Man
by Philip J Howard

MrH was 'The Middle Man' for some of the biggest underworld factions in the world of crime. For over twenty five years he was the link and negotiator to the deals. From an eighteen year old kid to middle age there is nothing in life he hasn't seen. His motto is "let nothing in life surprise you" Here is his true view of events that took him to deaths door and almost beyond to eventually changing his life around and making him the renowned Film and TV Director he is today.

A book and film being produced in 2015.

Ray Quinn – The highs, the lows, the record contracts, the money, the life.

**This Time Round
By Ray Quinn**

PERCY
PUBLISHING

Visit www.percy-publishing.com for more information.

Facebook: www.facebook.com/percypublishing

Twitter: @percypublishing

To Contact Kevin Paul
Find him on FaceBook
Or Twitter @kp_est78.